WESTONBIRT

Association News

2021

~ Bono malum superate ~

Westonbirt Association News 2021

Published in paperback and ebook by Hawkesbury Press 2021
Hawkesbury Upton, Gloucestershire, UK GL9 1AS
www.hawkesburypress.com

For further information about the Westonbirt Association,
please contact
Westonbirt School
Tetbury, Gloucestershire, UK, GL8 8QG
www.westonbirt.org

ISBN 978-1-911223-77-1

Also available as an ebook

British Library Cataloguing in Publication Data
A CiP catalogue record for this book is available from the British Library

Contents

Westonbirt Association Officers 2021

EXECUTIVE COMMITTEE

President & Honorary Secretary Mrs Leigh Ralphs
Honorary Treasurer Mrs Karen Broomhead
News Finances and Distribution Mrs Jenny Webb
News Editor Mrs Bridget Bomford
Headmistress Mrs Natasha Dangerfield
Staff Representative Mrs Joy Bell

Co-opted Members
Mrs Serena Jones
Ms Karen Olsen
Mrs Mary Phillips
Mrs Debbie Young

Support Roles
Membership Assistant Mrs Jane Reid
Head of Public Relations & Events Mrs Rhiannon Roche

GENERAL COMMITTEE

The Executive Committee and all the Section Representatives

2021 ANNUAL GENERAL MEETING

Saturday 16th October 2021

VICE PRESIDENTS

Mrs P Faust
Dr A Grocock
Mrs M Henderson
Mrs G Hylson-Smith
Miss Karen Olsen

HONORARY MEMBERS

Mr R Baggs
Mrs B Bomford
Miss V Byrom-Taylor
Miss D Challis
Mrs S Cole
Miss B D Cooper
Mr P Dixon
Mrs D Elsdon
Mrs S English
Mrs L J Evans
Miss M Evett
Mrs M R Farley
Mrs J Hutchings
Mrs V A Innes
Mrs R J Kingston
Miss J Marr
Miss E M Miller
Miss P E Morris
Mrs H Nickols
Mrs H Owen
Mrs J Paginton
Miss O T Pasco
Mr D Philbey
Mrs M Phillips
Mrs H R Price
Mrs A M Reed
Mrs J Reid
Mrs A Rodber
Mrs D Thombs
Mrs C Tilley
Miss S Urquhart
Mrs M Walding
Miss K S Yates
Mrs D Young

Editorial

As I sit here, starting this editorial, I have no idea what I am going to say. The year has been “unprecedented”, “like no other”, we are living in “strange times” and wondering about what the “new normal” will be, in a “post-Covid world”...We’ve heard it all ad nauseam.

Two years ago, if we heard a prediction of how life would change in 2020, we probably wouldn’t have believed it. Yet here we are, we have come through three lockdowns, many of us have not been able to see loved ones face to face for over a year, and some of us will have lost loved ones, myself included. Such experiences concentrate the mind, and make us reassess what’s really important...

As is to be expected, our younger members seem to have taken the changing circumstances into their stride and adapted well, partly because there are less responsibilities at this point in life. Inevitably, some plans have been put on hold for a while, but there are many examples of girls doing things they didn’t expect, like running pizza deliveries from a trailer, and working night shifts packing parts of Tangle Teezers (detangling hairbrushes – I had to look it up!). I think that’s a clear indication that Westonbirt produces resilient, fully-rounded young people, who are not put off by a mere global pandemic!

On a more serious note, I think the world, and the planet, are going to need as many resourceful and resilient young people as possible over the next few years. Life today offers opportunities and possibilities that only twenty years ago would have seemed impossible; but alongside these come responsibilities. For better or worse, in the world today information is ubiquitous and instant. In years gone by, things went on in the world, often bad or damaging things, that the general population knew nothing about. Had they known, the health and security of the world and the planet, might have been much better and safer than it is today. Young people in 2021 do not have the peace of mind that comes from ignorance, and consequently they have the burden of responsibility to put things right.

So, what’s really important? What do we really need? What are we doing to the planet? What should the future look like? Everyone will have their own opinions on these issues. But surely there are some basic truths to be learned here? Truths like treating everyone with the respect and kindness with which we would ourselves wish to be treated, truths like extending this respect and kind caring to our natural world, which sustains us, truths about the difference between want and need... Just because we **can** do something, do we really **need** to? Just because we **can** have something, do we really **need** it?

Well, one thing we do need, is young people of the very highest calibre to negotiate their way through to a better future for the world and the planet. And we need places like Westonbirt, places with a history and reputation for inspiring young minds, a flair for turning expectation on its head in positive ways, a place where every young person is given the support to reach their full potential. Westonbirt has had to change and adapt in order to survive, and it's doing this magnificently right now; it's become coeducational, and in September it will have its highest ever number of pupils on site. It's a transformational place, and transformation is the key to a better future.

Bridget Bomford

President's Report

As you are aware, because of Covid-19 we have had to postpone the Reunion on 22nd May 2021, for yet another year. As soon as we have a date for next May, we will let everyone know. Instead, the School emailed a video for alumni to watch. It was filmed by pupils and was an informal look at "A day in the life of a Westonbirt pupil" - which of course now includes boys!

In December, Rhiannon also sent out links to the "12 Doors of Christmas" which showcased pupils performing behind a variety of Westonbirt School doors. It was greatly enjoyed by many alumni in the festive run-up to Christmas.

During the various lockdowns, the Executive have remained busy and have held our meetings on Zoom. At our last meeting it was decided that we should try to have an AGM/GCM this year and so it will be on **Saturday, October 16th, 2021**. We appreciate that it is less than the 12 months' notice we usually try to adhere to, but in the current Covid situation we hope that everyone will understand that we are having to be very flexible. We also realise that not everyone will be able, or want, to travel to Westonbirt in these uncertain times, so the morning meeting will be available to attend by Zoom or in person, depending on your circumstances. For those who would like to go to Westonbirt, the School will arrange tours, lunch and Chapel as usual. We will be asking for numbers nearer the time.

We have also been discussing the proposal of a new Association Award for alumni which will be presented to the GCM/AGM at our next meeting, and we continue to explore ways for the Association to move forward, especially as the current Executive have been working tirelessly over many years and it's time for a change! My thanks as ever go to all of them for their wisdom, help and encouragement, to all the Section Reps for keeping in touch with their contemporaries and collecting in their news, and to Bridget Bomford and Debbie Young for editing it and putting it all together into this 2021 Association News magazine, available to buy through Amazon or Jenny Webb, for you all to enjoy.

I would also like to thank the Head, Natasha Dangerfield, for her continued support of the Association, Joy Bell, Assistant Head, for posting interesting news and photos on the Association's Facebook page and Rhiannon Roche, Head of Events, who helps with organising our activities and liaising with alumni.

Leigh Ralphs

Headmistress's Report

This year, the life in school has been like no other most of us have known. I am of course, acutely aware of previous Westonbirt experiences and many have likened parts of the experience to the disruption that the Second World War brought with it. Certainly, Westonbirt had to respond quickly to the request of the Air Ministry to take over the house and the school drew together to move swiftly to Bowood – an incredible time. Therefore, this is a complex alignment between the two time periods, and I am not sure that the situation quite warrants such a comparison. However, we will have managed some concerns from our parents, pupils and staff which undoubtedly in 1938 Miss Grubb would have dealt with too.

The storm of the pandemic has created the need for the school to attend to a variety of urgencies, but it has also, as we have found our way through the debris, determined some opportunities for us.

All of the staff and pupils have had to respond to a brand new method of teaching and learning online. Some of you, as parents, will have had to adapt to becoming a teacher! The shift to the digital classroom, although certainly an ask, had already been honed through the Summer Term lockdown, and we really enjoyed the opportunity to find more exciting elements of Zoom and Teams to incorporate into our successful teaching. Our numbers have grown, and this year we have had a coeducational Years 7, 8, 9 and 12. This September, not only will we see the highest number of pupils on site, but we will also see all years, bar Year 11, as a co-ed group and we have really enjoyed the shift.

Boarding numbers, as with the entire boarding school community, have dropped, and we will be working hard to rebuild here. Consequently, as we await further works, we will see original Badminton dormitories at the front of the main house, being converted to the Modern Foreign Languages department, and our first boy boarders will be descending in the area of Badminton to the east of the House. A number of the small dormitory rooms in the Sixth Form Stable block have been upgraded to create a day study centre for the Years 12 and 13, while the other half of this long 'Modern' corridor has become the Music Department – which, rumour has it, it once was!

A ten-year master plan is under preparation with architects, planners and English Heritage, which will bring some exciting regeneration which we will share with the Association once there is confirmation. Our relationship with HoWT continues very positively, and I am delighted that one of the key areas, the lake, is gloriously restored, with our sincere thanks to one of our wonderfully generous members of the Association. New silks in the Reading Room are at last hanging. We will share some pictures once it is all complete.

Our key values, which work within the concepts of '*greenhouse not a hothouse*', '*confidence without arrogance*' and '*inspiring young minds*' remain ever present, and I hope that your memories of your time here, however long ago, are pricked as you read through the narratives that follow. Once the 'roadmap' allows, please feel free to pop us on your destination list; we would love to welcome you back for a visit.

Mrs Natasha Dangerfield

School News

At this point, in recent editions, the Association News has included an update on how Association members have been involved with supporting Careers events at school, in many varied and interesting ways. Sadly, due to Covid, this has not been possible since 2019, although last year we were able to include an item on the literary week our own Debbie Young spent at Westonbirt, working with the English Department. This year, we have an alternative little item which we hope you will enjoy!

Second Generation at Westonbirt

The following piece has been written by **Sarah Pope**, whose daughter **Mary** joined Year 7 in September 2020. **Sarah (then Biddulph)** was a pupil at Westonbirt herself twenty three years ago:

Having looked at various other schools, our daughter, Mary, was very keen to go to Westonbirt, so after 23 years I am back there, dropping off Mary for her first day in Year 7. Very sadly with the year we have had we have not been able to get into school to see around but have heard plenty from Mary.

So has anything changed? The obvious things are the addition of boys and the new swimming pool on site which does not fill with leaves. There are also some new buildings, a new music block and upgraded English classrooms. There is plenty that has not changed, though. Mrs Bell and Miss Gould are both still very much at the heart of the school. Lacrosse is still part of school life, and luckily the main building and science labs have not changed. Mary is very much entering into the life at school, and it is good to know that the same ethos and spirit is still there.

Incidentally, Sarah Biddulph was a member of the very first cohort of Leith's students - so both Sarah, and Mary her daughter, have been taught by Mrs Bell!

Deaths Notified Since 2020

(cw = contemporary with: denotes a non-member's cohort)

Name	Section	Date of death
Mrs Elizabeth Bullingham	Staff	13 October 2020
Miss N Olwen Davies	Staff	20 June 2020
Prudence Helen Mennell (Vansittart)	11	24 March 2021
June Jacobs CBE (Caller)	17	22 July 2018
Sallie Hotchkin	19	1 November 2020
Elizabeth Noyce (Bale, Clark)	23	3 December 2020
(Carolyn) Jane Hopkinson (Milner)	24	9 August 2020
Elisabeth Abrahams	25	21 December 2020
Rhonwen Watts (Murray)	27	December 2021
Virginia (Gini) Anne Dowty	39	8 January 2021
Kofo Majekodunmi (Full married name Kofoworola Aduke Vigo)	42/43? (cw)	2 October 2020
Felicia Milicevic (Leman)	44	12 November 2020
Jane Seymour	45	8 December 2020
Jane Sinclair	46 (cw)	14 January 2021

Obituaries

Miss (Norah) Olwen Davies (1926 – 2020)

Norah Olwen Davies was born in 1926 and joined Westonbirt School at the age of 31, where she taught Mathematics and became the youngest Housemistress for Holford. Prior to Westonbirt she had achieved an MA at Edinburgh University followed by a Dip Ed at Oxford. She taught at a girls' Remand Home in Essex and Russell High School in Purley before spending four years as Deputy Headmistress at Woodford House in New Zealand. These were happy years and, particularly after retirement, she returned many times to visit New Zealand.

After eight years at Westonbirt, where she made an impression on many pupils (see comments below), she left in 1965 to become Head at St Mary's Hall, Brighton and then St Swithun's School, Winchester, before retiring. She stayed in touch with education, becoming President of the Girls' School Association in 1981 and also governor to several schools in Hampshire where she lived. She also interviewed for GAP, which sends students abroad for a year between school and university. She became an Honorary Member of the Westonbirt Association, and regularly kept in touch through the Association News.

Alison Gauld remembers Miss Davies with great affection:

"I first knew Miss Olwen Davies in September 1961 when she taught me Maths in Sedgwick. I immediately liked her. It seemed to me that we had very similar minds, logical and mathematical. She had been in New Zealand, and was now the housemistress of Holford, the youngest to be appointed as such. I was delighted a year later to be chosen to go into Holford House where she was in loco parentis.

"Whether we were naughty or good, Miss Davies always supported us to the hilt. She was firm, kind and had a good sense of humour. Many years later, when I asked her how she had dealt with difficult problems over her career, she said to me that there was nothing that a sense of humour couldn't help. How often after that have I been guided by those words of wisdom! After she left in 1965 to be Head of St Mary's Brighton, she continued to write to us, spurring us on in our GCEs and congratulating us afterwards.

"I caught up with Olwen in 1999, after she'd retired, as she lived nearby, with her nephew and family close by to support in her later years. Her nephew lived opposite her bungalow in Alresford, Hampshire, and his family was such a help to her in her later years. When I told her that I was thinking of offering my services as Old Girls' governor, she said that they would be lucky to have me. Any new achievement and she seemed as proud as a parent.

"To me she was a lifelong friend. I used to visit her in Alresford and take her out for lunch. She would come over to my house and the first time I was invited to hers I felt truly honoured. We discussed poetry. She liked U A Fanthorpe. We even knew each other well enough to discuss politics! Throughout her life she was a regular communicant and I have no doubt that her soul is now at peace after a truly exemplary life in service to others."

Other members of Westonbirt Association also remember her well:

Carol Mullin *"I wish I had not been a cringingly shy teenager when I had her as housemistress. I think I would have liked her a lot now. I can only remember one occasion when she summoned me for a private ticking off, and I suddenly realised she was a real, warm person with a very good sense of humour. It was a glimmer of the dawn of a much-needed courage or confidence, and it meant a lot to me. I remember her laughter. I would imagine she was a very good housemistress!"*

Barbara Workman remembers her as *"an excellent Maths teacher and genuinely likeable person."*

Jane Reid *"She was one of my teachers for double A Level Mathematics, and I enjoyed the lessons. I was the only one doing Maths A Level, and lessons took place in the Holford drawing room (enlivened once by a cat bringing in a live shrew, which she managed to catch and release outside on the terrace). She once commented to me that she could accept that my sister was not as good at maths as I was, but a teacher's life was easier if a pupil were consistent, and my sister had an unnerving tendency to get a very good mark, or a very bad mark."*

Karen Olsen *"I also remember Miss Davies as a good Mathematics teacher. She took about 20 of my year in the top division through O Level two terms early. She thought we were ready for the exam in the autumn term instead of taking it the following summer term. We all passed bar one,* *which shows what a good teacher she was - we were not by any means brilliant pupils!"*

Philippa Dutton *"I was at school with Miss Davies. She taught me Maths. Her brother was the conductor Meredith Davies. I left school in 1965. She was referred to as Noddy, I seem to remember, her initials being NOD."*

Katie Doorley *"Memories from my mum... She left in 1961. Miss Davies' birthday was mentioned in the* Daily Telegraph *over the last few years. She liked reading and borrowed my mum's books to read! Mum has her signature all over her school books, the girls had to have their books 'passed' to show they were reading suitable books for house members! Mum thought she was a good housemistress. When the girls had to do domestic chores, she would play classical music to them as they worked. My mum remembers her fondly."*

Miss Olwen Davies will be remembered as an excellent teacher and as a warm, caring and humorous individual. She will be missed.

June Jacobs (Caller) (1930 – 2018)

June Jacobs (Caller), a member of sections 17/18, was born in 1930 and educated at Westonbirt in the 1940s. **Joy Willey (Crowe)** saw her right up to the end of her life and says, `````````````

After leaving school, June married Basil Jacobs, a businessman then proprietor of an art gallery, who she had met when they were both volunteering at a boys' club in the East End of London.

Through voluntary involvement in a variety of communal organisations, she rapidly rose to take up leadership positions. Her activities included mobilising support for Jews in the Soviet Union, working for justice for Palestinians and Jews in the Middle East, defending the rights of asylum seekers and refugees in the UK, and working for equality for women throughout the world.

She became known as an advocate of Jewish Women's issues and was President of the International Council of Jewish Women from 1996 to 2002. She was appointed CBE in the 2009 Birthday Honours for her contribution to human rights and interfaith work.

(Compiled by Serena Jones and Joy Willey, using the following sources: obituaries from *The Guardian*, (03/08/18); *The Times* (15/08/18), and the *Daily Telegraph* (30/07/18); *The Jewish Chronicle*; and Wikipedia).

(Canon) Jane Sinclair (1957 – 2021)

A comprehensive obituary for Jane Sinclair can be found in the 29/01/21 edition of *The Church Times*.

Mrs Elizabeth Bullingham *(2/12/80 – 13/10/20)*

Joy Bell's tribute to Lizzie Bullingham on behalf of the whole school community appears on page 17.

SECTION NEWS

Thank You to Section Representatives

The Association is enormously grateful for the hard work and attention to detail shown each year by the Section Representatives, who volunteer to collect and collate the news from their former classmates. Modern technology makes this much easier than years ago, with many of even the most senior members sending in their news by email. Some members have also found social media, particularly Facebook and Twitter, useful for newsgathering.

Thank You to Association Members

We are always pleased to hear members' news, so if you're a regular respondent, thank you very much for continuing to keep us posted.

If you've not sent in your own news for a while, please don't hold back. Even if you feel you have nothing to report, we still like to know that you are alive and well, and that we have the right contact details for you. We also love hearing reminiscences about your own time at Westonbirt.

We have listed members in alphabetical order by their current surname, to make it easier to find your friends.

If reading any of their news makes you hanker after a nostalgic trip back to Westonbirt, we'd love to see you, when restrictions are eased and visits become possible. The annual Association Day is a great opportunity to meet up with old friends, and visits by appointment are welcome all year round. To arrange to visit, or for any information regarding the Association, such as the current contact details for your Section Rep, please do not hesitate to contact Miss Heather Barnes, PA to the Headmistress, via her school email address, heather.barnes@westonbirtschool.uk or by telephoning her on 01666 880333.

To Arrange a Visit or for Information

To arrange to visit, or for any information regarding the Association, such as the current contact details for your Section Rep, please do not hesitate to contact Mrs Rhiannon Roche, Head of Public Relations and Events, via her school email address, rroche@westonbirt.gloucs.sch.uk, or by telephoning her on 01666 880333

Staff Section

Section Representative:
Mrs Joy Bell

Chaplain's message – Rev Alice Monaghan

What does it mean to be a chaplain to a school that can't meet in person? How can we be in Chapel as a community when we have to stay 'bubbled' in our year groups and are not allowed to sing? How can we have carol services without carols and no parents or guests allowed? What is God saying to Westonbirt School through this unprecedented time? These are just some of the many questions that I have been wrestling with over the last year under the cloud of COVID 19 and the lockdowns.

I have often returned to a poem by Minnie Louise Haskins that our Queen gave her father, the King, when she was 13 years old, as he was on his way to give his Christmas message to our country three months into the Second World War:

I said to the man who stood at the gate of the year:
"Give me a light that I may tread safely into the unknown."
And he replied:
Go out into the darkness and put your hand into the Hand of God.
That shall be to you better than light and safer than a known way."

This encouragement and the words of the resurrected Jesus:

"I will be with you always, to the end of the age." (Matthew 28:20)

have spurred me on to preach about God's goodness and his steadfastness. So, as we enter the unknown of Life after Lockdown, I pray you will know God's presence with you.

In a slight departure from the norm, the next item has been specially written by Joy Bell, in tribute to Lizze Bullingham, a fantastic teacher and friend to many, whose sudden death shocked the whole school and wider community. Many recent Association members will remember Lizzie, but might not pick up a tribute in the Obituaries section, hence its inclusion here:

Rev Alice Monaghan

Mrs Elizabeth Bullingham

(2/12/80 – 13/10/20)

As a school community, we were devastated to learn, on the morning of 14th October 2020 that Mrs Elizabeth (Lizzie) Bullingham had died, suddenly at home, the previous evening, aged just 39.

She had joined the school as Miss Lizzie Cutts in 2008, to teach Spanish and French. She quickly proved to be an immensely caring teacher and tutor. She was well liked by both pupils and staff, and well respected throughout the school. For a number of years, she was Duke of Edinburgh coordinator, she ran a very successful jewellery making club (she had won prizes for her jewellery designs), and she also joined Mrs Gill to deliver the A Level Travel and Tourism course, drawing on her experience of living and studying abroad.

She set up and ran a number of language and culture trips to Spain as well as accompanying such trips to France. On one memorable occasion, due to staff illness, we needed a member of staff to accompany the lacrosse tour to the USA, and Lizzie stepped in at two days' notice.

She was an exceptionally dedicated and empathetic Lower School tutor, so it was a natural move for her to progress her career along the pastoral route by becoming Head of Lower School.

Lizzie married Jamie Bullingham in 2013, and we were delighted when their daughter Maisie was born in 2017.

Following maternity leave, Lizzie returned to Westonbirt in a part-time capacity. Her pastoral role was now Year 7 Coordinator, and her teaching developed in new directions. We needed a teacher to deliver the BTEC course in Children's Play, Learning and Development, and Lizzie relished this new opportunity, even bringing baby Maisie to school on occasion so that the students could see in real life what they were learning about. We also needed a specialist languages teacher for the prep school, and again Lizzie rose to this new challenge, putting great energy and enthusiasm into developing suitable content and resources to enable her to teach French and Spanish to all pupils from reception to Year 6.

Lizzie's death was a huge shock - she had not been ill. She leaves a huge hole in our community as well as in her family.

Reverend Alice was honoured to be asked to conduct the service for Lizzie at Westerleigh Crematorium. Due to Covid restrictions, there could only be 30 attendees, and so Miss Rogerson, Mrs Gill, Mrs Spyvee and I were pleased to be invited to represent the school community at the service. Mrs Downes (now retired to Cornwall, and a close friend of Lizzie) also attended.

Lizzie had a very caring nature and definitely a wise head – as well as a lively and wicked sense of humour! She was a very good friend to so many of us, and I for one will never forget her.

Joy Bell

Stephanie Barnes (Current Head of Sixth Form and teacher of Media Studies and English) Chloe Isabel Barnes was born on the 28th of April 2021 weighing a wonderful 10lbs and 10ozs. Steph gave birth at Bath Hospital after a relatively short labour. Chloe was brought to her new home on site at Westonbirt School and warmly greeted by her proud big brother Sam. Despite the unusual year, Steph and her husband Ben are delighted to be enjoying each day as a family of four.

Joy Bell I am writing this as we prepare to welcome all of the children back to Westonbirt. I say 'all' as a small number of both day and boarding pupils have remained on site, and of course the campus-dwelling staff have looked after them very well. We have just short of four weeks to complete the spring term and I am sure we will cram in as much as we possibly can! So, since our last news, I have had two periods of teaching from home and the children are now very familiar with my own kitchen. I have certainly enjoyed my 'Dolly Parton commute' ("tumble out of bed and stumble to the kitchen"!) and we have done lots of demonstration and cook-along lessons, and even some staff cook-along sessions in the evening. While I have been based at home, it has been lovely to connect more with where I live, get to know my neighbours more, and have time to explore further on my many and various dog walks. That said, I am so looking forward to the interactions and banter at school.

Bridget Bomford For me, 2020 was a truly terrible year, as I lost my Mum in August, under the most horrendous circumstances, and although she did not have Covid, her death was as a direct result of the pandemic. She was in the local hospital when it struck, recovering from pneumonia, receiving physio, and waiting for her care package upgrade, at which point she would go back home. Then, the hospital she was in had to be emptied so it could be used for Covid patients, so she was sent, temporarily, to a nursing home. (In fact, the hospital never did take Covid cases.)

To cut a long and awful story short, a resident at the home got Covid, and everyone was isolated. Mum kept testing positive, though she had no symptoms, so she remained in isolation for weeks. I'd got an iPad to her very early on, so was able to do Skype video calls with her, but she didn't really take to it, and each day, with her dementia spiralling appallingly, because of the isolation, there was less and less of my mum left. By the time she was allowed out of isolation (due to my involvement of Public Health England), her mental state had deteriorated so far that the damage was done, and she was no longer able to interact with other residents.

I did manage to go down (from Shropshire to Cornwall) and do six garden visits with her, but not being able to hug her or hold her hand, having to wear PPE and sit two metres apart, with her not really understanding why, was heart-breaking.

Then, a few days before my next planned garden visit, the home got another Covid case, and I was told I wouldn't be able to see her, which was shattering. A day or two later I was told Mum wasn't quite herself, was very sleepy, and not up to a Skype call. Things escalated rapidly from here on, with the GP at the home prescribing antibiotics for a chest infection, but within hours she was in hospital, the infection turned to sepsis, and in less than 24 hours Mum passed away, before I was able to get down to be with her. Words can't explain how devastating I found this.

So, we managed to have a funeral with 30 guests, and refreshments in the garden of the pub next to the church. Very fortunately my niece and nephew, from Norfolk and South Wales, were able to come.

I spent six weeks, on my own, clearing Mum's bungalow. She and Dad had moved there in 1992, but they had brought so much with them it was like clearing the family home. I was coming across so many things from my childhood, and things from both sides of my family dating back five generations. It was truly the most painful thing I've ever had to do. And I had no idea how hard it would hit me to no longer have a parent alive, or, for the first time in my life, not to have a place in Cornwall to call home.

I was very fortunate with the sale of the property as there was a local couple who were desperate to buy it and wanted it for all the same reasons Mum and Dad had. They love all the trees Dad planted, and Mum's garden, and the place will be a menagerie once again as they have miniature goats and sheep, horses, dogs, cats and ducks!

So, life has changed dramatically for me in the last year, and inevitably we have to move on. I'm still getting used to not having to go to Cornwall for a week every month, as I did over the last couple of years, and I'm so lucky to live here with Steve, in our little rural paradise. I do love it, and I will have more time now to create our wildlife haven, grow lots of veggies and enjoy all the fantastic birds and wildlife. I will always be a 'Cornish Maid', but I'm also becoming a 'Shropshire Lass'!

Diana Challis This has been a very strange year. I am keeping well but all the volunteering I normally do is on hold at present. I walk a lot and have explored areas around Tetbury that I hardly knew existed. I have learnt how to work Zoom and other aspects of technology, but they don't replace face to face contact. My Yorkshire cottage is somewhat neglected but I did manage to get there on several occasions last year between lockdowns. On the positive side I have formed a bubble with my sister, who lives not far from Tetbury, so we can visit in each other's houses ,which has been really good. I have now received my two jabs and hope for better times in the summer.

Sue Cole Not a lot of news for 2020, but I was lucky to spend a week in February, playing golf in Fuerteventura, where the weather was good, although for three days we couldn't see much because of the sandstorm which had blown there from Africa. In March, I also had a short golfing break in Cornwall. This was followed by the first lockdown, and I managed to stay sane doing my daily walk, Zoom Pilates, Zoom choir and Zoom coffee mornings. My house has never been cleaner and the garden looked really good!

Sheila Urquhart visited me just before lockdown, and when able to, I have seen **Mary Henderson, Ann Dunn, Jane Keay, Sarah Nannestad (Nutter), Gill Fry, Diana Challis** and **Helen Price**. I am in regular contact with **Gill Hylson-Smith.**

Beryl Cooper I am alive and well, which in itself is enough of a blessing when one is 91, and with good friends and a pleasant place to live. Mind you, I am not sure that the tattoo parlour which is just about to open round the corner from me is going to add greatly to my quality of life, but no doubt that is just prejudice.

Dee Francis Greetings from Chepstow! Lockdown here has meant we have to walk from home on our trips out - no driving! But the Wye Valley is a very beautiful place to live so we are very lucky.

Lots of walking, Zoom talking and trying to improve our French has filled our days, though we are looking forward to more freedom here in Wales very soon. First stop: the hairdresser!

Wishing all ex-colleagues good health and more freedom in the latter part of 2021.

Mary Henderson Almost a year into a lifestyle hitherto unimaginable, I confess that I have enjoyed having time, space and a virtually empty diary. Of course, I know how fortunate we are to live in relatively Covid-free Bath, to have a garden and allotment needing attention, and to be surrounded by beautiful countryside for daily walks.

I do miss golf and tennis, but we have managed to keep singing, after a fashion, via Zoom, and I have joined my first book club, also on Zoom, which is remarkably successful.

The Bath/Aix-en-Provence Twinning Association meets for monthly talks where for the first time our friends from Aix can join us live on Zoom. In June I am leading a discussion on *La Peste*, by Albert Camus, which fortunately is my favourite French novel. Rereading it has been very moving, especially as the parallels with the current pandemic are so poignant.

Walking in Scotland is always a highlight and last August **Chris Lloyd**, **Sheila Urquhart** and I enjoyed a week of wall-to-wall sunshine on Mull. I am banking on fine weather again this year with the same week on Mull, followed by a much-anticipated Nutter's Golfing Tour to Arran with Sheila, **Sue Cole** and **Sarah Nannestad** (née **Nutter**!).

I am relieved no longer to be anywhere near the chalk face at Westonbirt and greatly admire Natasha and her colleagues for "keeping the show on the road" so well during this challenging year. I gather that pupil numbers for September, both girls and boys, are spectacular, and I could not be more delighted!

Jill Hutchings It turned out that 2020 was not a good year to be celebrating our Diamond Wedding. Our planned party was of course not possible and the family weekend in Nice was cancelled. However, we managed to turn it into a low-key but very pleasant occasion, and instead of the south of France we went to Ludlow. Since the sun shone and the town is full of historic buildings and splendid places to eat, we had a thoroughly good time. Never have we been more grateful for a nice garden than during the summer. We were part of a village open gardens afternoon in September (before the latest lockdown) and on a lovely sunny day we had plenty of visitors who were glad to have somewhere local to go where they could meet (at a distance) with friends and exchange news. I have felt really sorry for everyone who has had to cope with distance learning and especially for those trying to make plans for further education. University life does not seem to be an attractive proposition at the moment. Let's hope for better things soon.

Gillian Hylson-Smith My biggest and saddest piece of news is that my husband died on February 2nd 2021, having had a very bad stroke six months before. We had been married for fifty nine years, and would have celebrated our Diamond Wedding in August.

Although my husband worked in Oxford he was a great supporter of Westonbirt, especially enjoying musical happenings and being a huge support to me personally. I miss him very much.

Sarah Nannestad I really appreciated living in the South Cotswolds with space in the house, a large garden and vineyard to keep us occupied, access to good walking, a village store and a pub geared for takeaway meals! Regular golf on the Westonbirt course (when permitted) keeps me in touch with **Mary Henderson**, **Sue Cole**, **Ann Dunn** and phone contact with **Sheila Urqhart**. Looking forward to the 2022 Reunion!

Mary Phillips I am afraid that I don't have anything really exciting to report, probably the case with many people. All I can say is that we are all well, although missing family and friends with the lockdowns. Our Westie puppy, Dalgleish, who is now eight months old, has been a real life saver, getting us out for walks every day and keeping everyone entertained. Once we are allowed to travel, we are hoping to go to the Yorkshire Dales to do some serious walking with said puppy, who will then be a year old.

I have been using Zoom a great deal for my junior Art Club and for teaching my adult group, and while it is not ideal, it is better than nothing. This last year has allowed me to do my own art work, which has been a real joy. My return to school, for another two-year stint, ended abruptly with the disruption of Covid, although I am pleased to say that the Art Department is in very good hands with Anna Gage, Amy Cooke and Lisa Bradbury. Hopefully, the day will come when we can all visit school to see a real live exhibition and meet friends.

Helen Price My only news is that Richard had a stroke in October just as we arrived in Cornwall for a fortnight's holiday. Luckily, he is recovering well. The lockdown has not affected us too much as Richard has been housebound until recently, and still can't walk far. All our normal activities have come to a halt, and I must admit I've enjoyed the easy pace, especially as time is spent looking after Richard. The days fly by and I never catch up with everything I hope to do in the day.

I walk occasionally with **Sue Cole**, see **Diana Challis** and **Judy Paginton** on Zoom occasionally, and chat to **Ann Dunn** and **Jill Hutchings**.

Sheila Urquhart I have been very lucky to be in the Scottish Highlands during the pandemic, although it did get very busy with motorhomes and wild campers over the summer, and single track roads proved quite a challenge to many.

I was fortunate enough to be able to go to the Isle of Mull with some former Westonbirt colleagues in August. We had a magical day on Iona and another trip to Staffa to visit Fingal`s Cave - I have never seen so many dolphins on the trip across, even the boatman was amazed.

Having spent much of the first lockdown in marvellous weather looking across to the Isle of Harris, I took myself there in November, where I was able to golf and beach walk at a very gentle pace.

I am very grateful to have been able to keep in touch with former colleagues and pupils on a regular basis by email, I'm too remote for Zoom, which I am very glad to be!

Debbie Young As a sociable type, spending most of the last twelve months shielding has been driving me nuts, even though I was already working from home, and with a retired husband, so the change was not as great as it might have been.

My daughter Laura, who was six years old when I left Westonbirt, is now in her last year at school, and one benefit of lockdown has been to spend more time with her before she takes off for university. She is studying English Literature, History and Sociology at A Level and has had conditional offers to read English Literature at Aberystwyth, Bangor, Cardiff, Oxford Brookes and Swansea. Not sure which she'll choose yet – tricky to make such a big decision without having been able to visit any of the places in person, though she has attended their virtual open days. She's planning a gap year to include work experience in the charity sector, a photography course, and travel.

My husband has been in DIY overdrive throughout the pandemic, building me a writing hut in the garden and a mezzanine floor and staircase (all from scratch) in the extension he built a few years ago.

By the time you read this, my seventh Sophie Sayers Village Mystery, *Murder Lost and Found*, will have been published. In this one, a dead body is found in the village school's lost property cupboard. It is inspired by having spent several years working in the office next to Westonbirt's lost property cupboard, where it often seemed a dead body might easily lurk undetected! I've also published a new novelette (about a quarter the length of one of my novels) called *The Clutch of Eggs*, for which I did lots of enjoyable research about birdwatchers, wild birds' eggs and the biology of eggs – far more fascinating than I expected! All my books are available in ebook and paperback, and I'm starting to turn them into audiobooks too. Next on my list of books to write is *Scandal at St Bride's*, the third in my boarding school mystery series. I am having great fun!

Normally my calendar is full of events, but of course these have all been postponed or moved online. Having bought my first Senior Railcard last year, I have not had a chance to use it! I am doing a lot of competition judging, however, which can be done from home, this year for the Scottish Association of Writers, the Gloucestershire Writers' Network and Stroud Short Stories. I'm glad to see the latter half of my 2021 diary starting to fill up. I'm thrilled to have been invited to host a literary lunch at the Hilton Doubletree in Cheltenham on Sunday 12th September, which will feel like a real celebration after so long in lockdown. Details will be available on my website a bit nearer the time.

If you'd like to know more about my books and writing events, you can find out all about them and read the opening chapters of each book at my website: www.authordebbieyoung.com. I'm also on Facebook at @AuthorDebbieYoung, on Twitter as @DebbieYoungBN, and on Instagram as @DebbieYoungAuthor. It would be great to connect with Association members there.

NEWS FROM SECTION MEMBERS

Section 89 (2020)

Section Representative:
Eloise Stokes

No news returned this year

Section 88 (2019)

Section Representative:
Natia Jikia

No news returned this year

Section 87 (2018)

Section Representative:
Georgina Billingham

Holly Blundell I am currently finishing my last term at Bristol University, studying English Literature. I had originally planned to travel for a couple of years around South America, then onto Asia, Australia, and New Zealand, but for obvious reasons I've decided to put that idea on hold! Instead, I am going to move to London in the summer with friends, to work until I can travel again.

Georgina Billingham I am currently in my third of four years at Bath Spa University studying Business Management with Marketing. My course was originally a three-year course with a placement year, but because of Covid my placement was cancelled and the year was turned into a fourth year. Learning online has had its challenges, but mostly it has been alright, having lectures through Zoom or Google Meets, and while it would have been nice to have gone into uni and seen people, I didn't need to, and, luckily, I didn't miss out on too much.

While at university I have been working part-time at a pub in Bath since 2018 and have kept it up throughout; I was promoted to supervisor in December 2019. Unfortunately, I haven't been doing anything exciting over the past year, but we are looking into holidays and things to do, hopefully in the summer.

Bonnie Fairgrieve I am in my third and final year at Royal Holloway University, studying English Literature. It's been a very strange experience being taught completely online, but I think everyone is getting the hang of it now. I am filling all of the extra time with my course reading, as well as expanding my culinary skills by cooking for the family once a week and teaching my dad some recipes too. I am now the Vice President of the Rounders Sports club and have made many good friends through this: we have a weekly team games night on Zoom to keep in touch with each other through lockdown. I am also overjoyed and very excited to become an auntie to a baby girl in May.

Ella Morrison Despite the pandemic, the last year or so hasn't been all bad. I'm now in my third and penultimate year at the University of Bath on their BBA (Bachelor of Business Administration) course which I love. I completed my first round of industry experience at EY (Ernst and Young) along with a summer legal internship at Manchester United FC. In February of 2021 I started my second round of industry experience at the wealth management firm Brewin Dolphin. I was meant to be in London working from the office, but, due to the pandemic, have been working online from home. I will graduate in July 2022 and from there I want to go on to start my own business – which I won't bore you all with - haha. Or, alternatively, go onto become a qualified solicitor through a training contract scheme. I have started applications for this and hope to be successful - fingers crossed!

Outside of university, I've been enjoying picking up at numerous shoots with the dog – recently bought a puppy so that I can continue to do so with the hope of field trialing in the future. I have also been enjoying doing more painting (I've been lucky enough to undertake commissioned work which I hope will continue into the future.)

I hope you're all doing ok despite the catastrophic last year.

Francesca Napper Luckily for my set at Norland, we only missed out on one day of teaching before College closed in March due to Covid (one week early). My parents then picked me up from Bath the night lockdown was confirmed at about midnight to bring me home where my cousin Octavia and her best friend Freddie were already, as they were visiting from London for (what was supposed to be) a couple of days. Luckily, they brought extra clothes just in case lockdown happened!

As our residential placement couldn't go ahead, we did a virtual placement where we were given a family and told bits and pieces about them and had to plan meals and complete a nanny diary for them. We were sent observations to do, and twice-weekly scenarios of what our virtual charges were up to.

It was really nice having Octavia and Freddie with us for lockdown as I didn't really know them before (as they are ten years older than me). It was very helpful having Freddie around as he is a hairdresser! Some memorable moments during the first lockdown were a rounders match in a field mid dog walk, and another a spontaneous water fight in the garden! It was also nice to spend so much time with my parents, who obviously couldn't work. Dad kept himself busy (with Freddie's help) turning one of the ponds into a sunken vegetable garden and then got to work insulating the fridge, with no actual knowledge or instructions of how to do so!

Freddie also started teaching me how to drive. I can highly recommend learning to drive during lockdown, as there is nobody on the roads!

After Freddie went back to work in June, Octavia ended up giving up her flat in London to save money as she will be working from home for the foreseeable future. She moved back to London into a new flat in January.

I went back to Norland in September and did my residential placement with a lovely family - definitely my favourite placement, and not just because we had post-dinner dance parties to *Moana*!

Norland have a lot of risk mitigation measures in place so it feels very safe, even during the second lockdown we were still doing 80% face to face teaching. I came home on 9th December and have been online learning form home since then. I have also completed three-fifths of my third year degree assessments, including two-thirds of my dissertation. It's crazy to think all I have left to do is four more weeks of degree/diploma lectures, my final placement (a residential in February/March with three children) and then six weeks of employment lectures until I have finished college and start applying for jobs and start my NQN year!

Izzy Sach Since leaving Westonbirt I have been studying Geography at the University of Sussex and am graduating this year. I am currently looking at jobs in the development, environment and politics sector. Last March I took part in the Bath half marathon and raised money for MIND, but have not done anything really exciting (due to Covid) apart from some work experience in the summer. I am currently doing my dissertation on the Cotswolds and the rural idyll. Thank you to everyone at Westonbirt who helped me pursue my love for human geography. I can't wait to see friends from our year group when we can!

Christine Sun I am currently planning my final year graduation lab project, but I am still not sure when it will start. This is my third year at Nottingham University doing Chemistry. In the beginning, I did not get into the course I wanted, but now I am enjoying it and I am willing to take a step further. I have applied to several universities for a postgraduate course to do Chemistry in November and I am glad that I have received an offer from IC (Imperial College London), Sheffield, and Leeds. This is an approval for my ability and a great encouragement during this hard time. I also received an offer from Edinburgh on the day of Chinese New Year, which was a great gift during the time. However, they withdrew my offer the next morning and said it was a technical error which I think is an interesting and special experience. After some consideration, I accepted the offer from IC just a few days ago, so I am moving to London this September which is exciting and a little bit nerve-racking.

Kate Willey I'm currently in the final semester of my Political Science degree at Leiden University in The Hague, and putting the finishing touches to my dissertation on post-conflict reconstruction. In May, I was elected to the University Council, so have spent the past year writing and reviewing on various policies from Covid response to inclusion of international students - an excellent way to end an incredible three years in the Netherlands. I've also been in contact with fellow 'old girl' **Vanessa Newby** (Section 58) who teaches at Leiden and who I found through the Association News. We may be small, but there are Westonbirt girls just about everywhere if you look hard enough!

Section 86 (2017)

Section Representative:
Thea Montanaro

Suzanna Battishill Having graduated in the spring, I have enjoyed some time off before going on an adventure of a ski season with **Millie** to the Alps. I am hoping to do a summer season, and then perhaps back to Morzine next winter.

Cordie Cross After thinking I had finally finished with education, I decided over the summer to stay in Southampton another year and am now half way through doing my MA in Visual Communication at Solent. So far it's been going well, and despite the difficulties of doing a creative course during the pandemic, it's been really enjoyable. Looking forward to hopefully a fantastic summer when I can finally catch up with the girls. Sending lots of love and well wishes to all the Westonbirt community!

Lottie Dickens After my second ski season being cancelled due to Covid, I have been working back at home. However, I have just secured a job working for Winkworth in South Kensington and start after Easter.

Camilla Edwards Yet again just finished another ski season, this time with **Suzie B**. Just applied to become a French resident, so let's see what happens next!

CJ Egerton Living the software dream working in London. The capital is incredible and living alone has taught me, if anything, how to really vacuum an apartment. Love my job, and, can't lie, loving life - although it's agreed a few of us miss the study centre and Pizza Planet every now and again.

Kristie Fitzmaurice I enjoyed my three years at Cardiff whilst completing my undergrad so decided to stay another year to do an MSc(Econ) in International Relations. I will finish in October.

Isabelle Gent Currently finishing my final year studying music at Oxford Brookes. My plan is to have a gap year and find a music internship in London when I'm finished.

Thea Montanaro I'm pleased to have graduated with a First from Nottingham last summer. I had planned a year of travel but unfortunately Covid got in the way. Instead, I've been working at Tesco whilst applying for grad jobs. I also work on a pizza trailer, driving round to different locations and selling pizza, which is great fun.

Maureen Njeama I'm currently in my sophomore year majoring in Biology. So far it's all going pretty well, I'm doing human anatomy this semester, and am so lucky to be in a university where undergrads are able to work on cadavers. We get three cadavers in a semester and we have to dissect everything, and we get tested at the end of each week. I just got awarded the Research Assistant position for the second time this year, which is amazing, I'm also a Mentoring Ambassador.

Life over here is pretty busy, but I love it. It keeps me on my toes and constantly on the ball. I'm currently working on a new project with the school to try and get the leftover food from the canteen to go to non-profit organisations, so that's been keeping me super busy but working through it!

Very much missing Westonbirt! I feel like I learnt and took so much from the school, it's amazing to look back and reminisce on the good/crazy times with my girls!

Jessie Padday I decided to take a year out of university during the pandemic and I'm hoping to transfer to the University of the West of England (UWE) to study Fine Art in September.

Hanniel Phillips I had the most intense 2020, I'm sure we all did, but in the midst of it all, despite the pandemic, I had a really great year. I graduated from university, and I've gone on to start my master's programme at the University of Westminster in Human Resource Management, and I've also moved to London.

Sophia Rossi After a very difficult year in 2019, I went on a ski season in Meribel and had all of the fun I missed in 2019. The perfect place to recover and grow again. I am now back at Exeter University and enjoying myself as much as the pandemic will allow me. Surprisingly Percy the pug is still alive.

Emma Scott I am reaching the end of my third year of university, and am really enjoying writing my dissertation, which is about the music used on the early modern stage around the beginning of the seventeenth century. We have all adapted reasonably well to the online teaching, and while it is obviously not the same, some pretty fun things have come out of it too. For example, our Dante expert has taught us the proper way to make a martini. Apparently, you very definitely do not shake it. This seems important knowledge to be graduating with.

Kiera Segrave-Daly Enjoying my final year as an undergrad at Leeds, planning to stay here next year and study for a master's too. I have mostly been working on my dissertation but also written some articles for *The Tab* (multi-university youth news site) which I'm excited about.

Hannah Segrue I'm currently finishing my third year at the Royal Agricultural University studying food production and supply management. I'm hoping to secure a job in recipe development or new product development. Throughout lockdown I have been focusing on my dissertation and other uni work as well as going on lots of walks with friends.

Hunny Swain-Granger Throughout the pandemic I've been working in Bristol as a mental health care assistant alongside my degree. Covid has proved to put a huge strain on the NHS mental health services. It has been hard work but very rewarding and I've met some incredible colleagues along the way. Looking forward to having a boogie with my girls once this lockdown lifts!

Sharon Yu I'm still down south in Brighton and trying to complete my final year of education, the master's has been hard, but I'm just managing, and there's not long to go now until it's done. Would be nice to see everyone again after lockdown... missing you girlies always.

Section 85 (2016)

Section Representative:
Charlotte Price

Sophia Ashe Arrived back in the UK in May after spending eight months away working in Australia and Argentina. Got stranded in Argentina because of Covid but luckily was repatriated. Worked for a local farm contractor over the summer doing the harvest and have worked for him as Farm Administrator since autumn.

Maddie Hudson I've been completing my PGCE year training to be a secondary English teacher. I've been able to work throughout the pandemic, which makes me feel very lucky. It's been great to work in the classroom with keyworkers' children as well as trying to adjust to online teaching, but on track to get the qualification in June. I spend most of my time at home enjoying walks with my puppy, who has brought so much joy in such a tough time.

Ellie Parsonage Graduated from Falmouth University in June and is currently working for a small clothing brand as a designer.

Freja Petrie I'm doing a PhD looking at concussion prevention in women's rugby and have moved to a flat by the seaside with my boyfriend.

Charlotte Price is currently in Cambridge working for Cambridge University. She has recently been recognised throughout the university through the Alison Traub Assistant award, which selected her from over 500 assistant staff. Alongside her work she has set up a cookie business @cookiesby_char and is successfully running her bakery from home.

Fran Quince recently bought a flat in Cheltenham, moving back to start her new role with a tax accountant. Coinciding with her new job, she has undertaken various challenges for charity, one of which involves a 27-mile run in March 2021.

Hannah Reichwald I am currently living in Falmouth after graduating in the summer. I am teaching English as a second language online. I have set up my own theatre company, A Thing or Two Theatre, and we work closely with the Cornish community with the aim of destigmatising mental health.

Allegra (Jane) Seymour graduated with a First Class honours degree from Kingston School of Art having studied Fine Art and Art History. Since graduating, she has now founded her own sustainable clothing business that is featured on ASOS Marketplace, as well becoming verified as a Depop Top Seller. You can find some of her designs on Instagram: @madebylegs!

Section 84 (2015)

Section Representative:
Stephanie Thorndyke

Ella Frowen was excited to say that she has set up a catering company.

Kelsey Heath said that since graduating from University and Quest Professional, she moved into a studio apartment in Hammersmith. She loves living in London. She had a great job but Covid complicated things. So now she is actively searching for new employment.

Evie Jones is currently working night shifts 10pm-6am at a factory, sorting and packing parts of Tangle Teezers (detangling hairbrushes). She is still on furlough from Dirty Bones, the Oxford the cocktail bar and restaurant she was managing. She got a promotion from her part-time role there as a host when she graduated last summer with a first in International Hospitality Management. She was hoping to go into events/festivals so took the promotion instead because of the Covid situation at the time. She is now planning on moving to Barcelona in August - not sure what job yet but is moving with some friends and wants to improve her Spanish and would love some sunshine!

Phoebe Lowes In the last couple of years I've been travelling and having an amazing time in Australia and New Zealand, working and living there for six months, due to Covid. I came back early to find a "proper" job but as we all know it hasn't been the best year for all of that, but I am now employed (since October) with a high-end furnishing company called De Gournay, here in Wiltshire, and I am in charge of shipping clients' orders, SKOs and samples around the world, along with other duties. I'm loving it and have a great team around me, so the hours fly by! I keep in contact with **Kelsey Heath** and **Tilly White** and look forward to the day we can all see each other again!

Immy McTear wrote to say that she is living and working in London for a PR agency, but doesn't have any other news.

Elizabeth Motley I'm still living in London and working as a videographer, editor and social media content creator for a media and marketing company. In my spare time, I freelance for *The Honey Pop*, a global online music magazine, which allows me free front-row tickets to photograph gigs. Despite Covid preventing me travelling to Paris and Stockholm for work, I managed to fly to Dusseldorf to film for Steinway & Sons. I still keep in touch with **Tomi Lijadu, Laura Heenan**, **Louise Nichols** and **Amelia Schiller**."

Stephanie Thorndyke I have been on furlough since the pubs closed as I am a Kitchen Shift Leader. It has been a long time coming but I am looking forward to having some order back in my life. Being off work has allowed me to work on my mental health, slowly getting there and making (some) healthy choices! My plans for the near future are to move back home for a bit, find a new job (preferably in HR) and do some 'catch up' travelling... and of course to see friends and family and have a do-over on this past, lost year!

Charlotte Whitwham says that she changed employment and now she works for the Student Loans Company, in particular Student Finance England - an organisation with whom many people will be familiar! She works in the Undergraduate Funding Department and is gearing up ready for applications for funding for 21/22 academic year to be released in March. In terms of study herself, she is hoping to secure a place studying Mental Health Nursing at either the University of the West of Scotland or Glasgow Caledonian for her second degree.

Section 83 (2014)

Section Representative:
Amelie Sievers

Sophie Cork I finished my post-graduate Law degree remotely in June and started working as a trainee solicitor in September 2020. I am currently doing a secondment as part of my training contract at the Nursing and Midwifery Council, advising on fitness to practice cases, which I have found really interesting so far. I am now living in Reading with **Izzy Mathias** and we have been adding to our houseplant collection!

Bryony Curry I've been awarded the International Doctoral (PhD) Fellowship at the University of British Columbia (Okanagan) in Canada and I began my studies in Comparative Physiology last September. My boyfriend and I will be moving out there this summer and we're really excited!

Jessica Honer I am still working at the same distribution company as Head of Social Media and PR. During the pandemic we have undergone a re-brand in which I have been heavily involved on the marketing side, and it has enabled me to be very creative! My girlfriend Chloe and I have also recently bought our first house together, so we are very excited about moving ready for the summer!

Emily McGuire Over the last year I made my copywriting business full time and I'm loving it! It's bringing amazing opportunities - from publishing a copywriting guide, to being a part of a limited edition Prada book. I've since moved to Devon and am looking forward to the future.

Amelie Sievers After graduating from Exeter I moved back to Germany and am currently doing my master's in Business Psychology. Alongside, I am also doing a traineeship in Human Resources Management, with a focus on recruiting and talent acquisition, which means life is rather busy but really loving it and learning a lot!

Alice Wordsworth With the theatre industry thrown into crisis like the rest of the world, 2020 took a rather different turn for me. I finished my role as Resident Assistant Director at the Unicorn Theatre and received a Distinction in my Master of Fine Arts in Theatre Directing from Birkbeck. I have continued to teach my Young Company at the Rose Theatre remotely, and have also started a nannying job for three delightful French children in Regent's Park. Most excitingly, my theatre company set up a podcast called Stuck for Ideas. We interview creatives about where they go when they are stuck for ideas and have had an array of wonderful guests from Anna Winger, maker of hit Netflix show *Unorthodox*, to fashion photographers for Vogue. With over 3,000 downloads and press in *Hello* it has been a great success in what has been a rather slow year.

I am still living in London with the wonderful **Georgie Fenn,** and we have a new addition to our household - Bhala a three month old cockapoo! He has been a bundle of joy.

Sally Yau I am working as a pharmacist at Boots and as a clinical supervisor at ExCel London, helping out at the Covid vaccination centre. I am also studying clinical nutrition part time.

Section 82 (2013)

Section Representative:
Abi Lowes

No news returned this year

Section 81 (2012)

Section Representative:
Olivia Birkin-Hewitt

Olivia Birkin-Hewitt I am still living in Chippenham and working at RWBA (the secondary school in Royal Wootton Bassett). It's been an interesting year learning how to teach and assess students remotely, but also nice that I've been able to spend some time decorating and furnishing my new house (moved in September 2019).

I still keep in touch a lot with **Laura Green** and **Daisy Newman** - via virtual games or movie nights, and meeting up when we can. This lockdown would have been a lot harder without those two!

Tori Cowan Over the last year, I have managed to up my game, mostly thanks to Covid. I managed to set up my multi-consultancy, Peppergrass Consulting, using my many different experiences, from my two degrees, numerous project management qualifications, and one of my hobbies. I offer consultancy services in marketing, project management, efficiency management and land management. Focusing on, but not limited to, rural businesses, Peppergrass is a brand new, but fast-growing multi-consultancy.

I was also the luckiest person in the world, when my best friend asked me to marry him after five and a half years together. We were living in Oxfordshire at the time, and he took a day off from the farm on my birthday, took me on a picnic to the top of the Ridgeway, and asked me to spend forever with him! By the time the next one of these comes out, I will be Victoria Purton (still deciding if we double-barrel!). We get married later this year, on 18th September in Stanton St. Quintin, Wiltshire.

I also hear from **Fran Schiller** who is due to get married in June (fingers crossed). She's still living in London with Will, working hard and being as wonderful as she always was at school!

I don't hear much from many others in our year so if you're reading this, do get in touch - it would be so nice to hear from you. Especially as 2022 will mark 10 years since we left! Anyone up for a post-Covid reunion?

Section 80 (2011)

Section Representative:
Emily Clare

Diana Brain I left Westonbirt and went to Edge Hill University to study Film and TV Production. Three incredible years later, I passed with a high 2:1!

After that, I was ready to try breaking into the film industry, which has been way more difficult than first anticipated. A long time later, I eventually landed my first job working on the day time TV programme, *Dickinson's Real Deal.*

I got a few days on the set of a very big American costume drama called *Will.* You learn first-hand just how cutthroat the industry actually is, but, slowly, I started to get more work. This has led me to work on things such as: *The Festival, Vanguard, COBRA: Season 1, Everybody's Talking About Jamie, Master of None: Season 3* and *The Dark Crystal: Age of Resistance,* to name a few.

Currently, I've just finished something for Amazon Prime and moving on to a large BBC series in London. I have also stepped up a few times to become a 3rd Assistant Director, but hopefully to step up more permanently this year. During this time, I have done quite a bit of travelling, from all over Europe to Canada, China and Japan, which has been absolutely incredible!

Along the way I've met some of the most amazing, inspiring people and made lifetime friendships that have led to some very unique and extraordinary experiences I will always remember.

Sophie Cattermole I will be getting married this October (should have been October 2020) and I am also expecting a baby boy in early April, so it's going to be a busy year for us!

Emily Clare I'm living in London and still working in property. I got married last year (we were lucky our date in July was a dip between the lockdowns) I also watched every single episode of Keeping up with the Kardashians (that's 89 hours).

Rebekah Heaney Since moving back to the UK from the UAE a couple of years ago I've been working as a freelance writer, specifically as a ghost writer of science fiction and fantasy novels, while living in the beautiful Surrey countryside.

Georgina Hone I work at Foster and Partners, a world-renowned architecture firm. I have been working there for five years come May this year. I am a Senior Cover PA, and I am loving it there. I live in London, and am aspiring to buy my own gaff like the rest of us who haven't already done so. I am not with man or with child, and loving my late twenties of fun...aside from last year…and the beginning of this year…

Georgina Lee I moved with John up to North Yorkshire, between York and Malton, at the start of the first lockdown, as a family of four. Amongst the madness of Covid, I was very fortunate to find a job working as a Montessori teacher close by where my children also attend. We're also going to be becoming a family of five come mid-August, which both John and I are eagerly anticipating; this means we will have three children under the age of four! I am very much looking forward to what the next ten years holds for us all.

Tiffany Leung I am now in Hong Kong and working in my family business.

Alicia Motley This year I've inhaled my weight in Milky Bar Buttons and re-watched *The Office* for the 15th time.

Caroline Railston-Brown This year I've had to postpone our wedding, but we're hopefully moving into Josh's and my third home (we sold and moved on, not kept all three!) which we will refurbish from its original 60s design. I'm still a senior sustainability consultant in the construction industry and a chartered environmentalist. I have also started to watch *Sex and the City* again for the millionth time and I've never been happier.

Alice Steel I have been watching every episode of *Love Island* from Season 1, Episode 1.

Chawadee Sriprasert After I graduated with a bachelor's degree in Biochemistry from Imperial College London (2014), I decided to come back to Thailand to study medicine. After six years in medical school, I am now working as an intern at a hospital in Chiangmai, a province in Northern Thailand. Although working as a healthcare worker during Covid-19 has its challenges, I have definitely been enjoying the country life in Chiangmai. It is far less busy than Bangkok. It kind of reminded me of the old days in Tetbury!

As for the next year three years, I'm planning to go back to Bangkok for my residency in family medicine.

Section 79 (2010)

Section Representative:
Sophie Martin

No news returned this year

Section 78 (2009)

Section Representative:
Amy Falkenburg

No news returned this year

Section 77 (2008)

Section Representative:
Portia Ingram

Sophia Barker Sophia is still working for Malvern College, Hong Kong. She is really enjoying living there and experiencing another culture. Sophia is enjoying hiking regularly and exploring what the city has to offer. She hopes that everyone is keeping mentally and physically well during the Covid outbreak.

Mary-Jane Collinson Mary-Jane (Mudge) is now a GP registrar with an interest in elderly and lifestyle medicine, working in a rural GP practice in the Yorkshire Dales.

Portia Ingram Portia is working as an Executive Assistant within the financial industry in London. Having spent the past year working from home in Putney, she is looking forward to returning to the office and meeting up with lots of the Westonbirt girls again! She moved in with her boyfriend, James, last year.

Lucy Matthews (Clare) Lucy has been teaching Year 3 at a primary school in Cardiff for the past couple of years and this year she joined the board of governors. She is also completing a master's in Education Policy and Practice at Cardiff Metropolitan University. Her children, Amelia and Ben, are growing up far too quickly!

Charlotte Mayland (Sharland) Lottie is expecting her first baby in May and currently living in Dorset while she and her husband are renovating their house in south-east London. During lockdown Lottie set up a hand-embroidery business and now creates embroidered linens which she sells through Instagram and her website. She still counts the friends she made at Westonbirt as some of her closest friends and sees many of them regularly.

Tessa Oliver (Moreland) Tessa is currently working as a teacher in Oxford and living in a newly-renovated house in Henley. She is very excited to meet up with all the Westonbirt girls when lockdown is over.

Section 76 (2007)

Section Representative:
New Representative needed
(Report from Jane Reid – Section 30)

There were no replies from any of the six members for whom email addresses are held.

Section 75 (2006)

Section Representative:
Charlotte Boyes

No news returned this year

Section 74 (2005)

Section Representative:
New Representative needed
(Report from Jane Reid – Section 30)

There were no replies from any of the nine members for whom email addresses are held.

Section 73 (2004)

Section Representative:
Emily Paul (Stephenson)

No news returned this year

Section 72 (2003)

Section Representative:
Carey Milsom (Logan)

No news returned this year

Section 71 (2002)

Section Representative:
Joanna Colson
No news returned this year

No news returned this year

Section 70 (2001)

Section Representative:
Catharine Loveridge (Hallpike)

No news returned this year

Section 69 (2000)

Section Representative:
Lucy Croysdill (Fletcher)

Lucinda Davy (Dungarvan) I continue to work for a family office-based in Mayfair, which focuses on investment. I live in West London, married to Rory, a naval architect. Our daughter Tatiana is now two-and-a-half years old, a lot of fun, wonderful character, with a healthy serving of attitude!

Eila Denaro (Greaves) I, and our three boys, Rowley, Wilbur and Humphrey, spent a year living in Herefordshire (July 2019-July 2020) while James was deployed to Afghanistan. It was a blissful break from military quarters and patch life, made extra special by enjoying time with the grandparents and country life, and rekindling a very special friendship with **Hannah Lister (Leadbetter),** who was also in Herefordshire during that time.

James returned from abroad and we promptly moved to Aldershot, where we will now be for the next couple of years. Humphrey joined his older brothers at school in September and the house was suddenly rather quiet between 9am and 3pm.

I have continued with my small but busy curtain and interiors business when I'm not running around after a new puppy and the boys.

Longing for that cancelled reunion to happen and to see people again...

Lucy Fletcher (Croysdill) We have kept busy and well this year. Missing seeing friends and family. I was kept well occupied with work and home schooling Nina, now eight and in Year 3, during the lockdowns. Lots of time spent outside exploring new walks around our area in Tunbridge Wells and were thankful for the lovely weather we had. We managed a quick visit to see **Henny Mercer (Vickery)** in France last summer, and even though we had to quarantine on our return to the UK it was worth it as we had a fantastic week with her! Sad not to see everyone at the reunion last May but looking forward to next year.

Katie Fortune (Wennink) We have been really lucky over the last year that both myself, Donald and Rufus have been well and that we have managed to weather lockdown and survived all that it has entailed. I have managed to keep teaching, even if it is over bloody Zoom! (I hate screens at the best of times, but the kids have been amazing!) Donald has managed to keep building (I think all households now want their washing machines silenced and hidden and new extensions built so families can escape each other!) and Rufus, at the tender age of two-and-a-half, is as feral as ever, but his happiness and ability to be very much in the moment has kept us all busy and our spirits up!

Potty training is soon to be in the mix with puppy training. Cassie, my lovely dog of fifteen-and-a-half-years sadly passed away in February, so the Wennink Pack is to have a new member joining us in April, so I'm sure that will keep us busy for a while. Fingers crossed we may even get to head back up to the Highlands to run on some beaches.

I start working at Thomas's Battersea as well as Clapham, where I currently work as one of their senior Learning Specialists come September. The irony of me being an undiagnosed dyslexic at school and now working as a dyslexia specialist still makes me giggle and slightly hold my breath! Just shows you anything is possible. I hope that everyone else has been well and the losses haven't been too great for all. Our friends and families and health are what really count, and slowing down is sometimes what we need. Much love to everyone. xxx

Laura Griffiths (Arnott) Living in Alexandria, Virginia. Staying home with my three children (6, 4 and 1). Home schooling is hard! We've added two cats to our family this year in the Covid madness. Really missing our family and friends in the UK.

Lucinda Hennessy Since getting engaged to my partner, James, in February 2019, I am delighted to announce the birth of our daughter, Sophia Elodie, who was born in May 2020. We were over the moon at her arrival. We unfortunately had to postpone our wedding due to the pandemic, but we are hoping to get married in the near future.

Hannah Leadbetter (Lister) Moved to Virginia Beach in the USA back in July and although we have been slightly restricted due to Covid we have still managed to see a lot and taken advantage of being near ski slopes in the winter. Summer is now 7 and Halle 4. They have settled well at school and nursery out here and are enjoying the adventure. Halle starts school in September and is very excited. We are due to return to the UK in 2022 and will be moving back to our home in Dorset.

Henrietta Mercer (Vickery) Very sad not to catch up with 'old' friends at the Westonbirt reunion but hoping to see you all in 2022. Living in the South of France with my husband and three-year-old twins. Starting my new role as Deputy Head of the International School of Monaco and Class 3 teacher in September. Hoping to see many more friends and family this year if possible!

Poppy Morgan (Moll-Morgan) We are back from our year in Mallorca, and settled in Sussex just before the pandemic. I have since set up a new business, Felt Creative, that specializes in creating home decor wooden items adorned and filled with felt balls! It has been a ball (pardon the pun) and has done well enough to enable me to leave my job to focus on it this summer. I have made a number of boarding house names for High Wycombe and a couple of private schools in Switzerland and Dubai. I am hoping to start selling with Not on the High Street later this year.

Section 68 (1999)

Section Representative:
New Representative needed
(Report compiled by Jane Reid – Section 30)

There were no replies from any of the thirteen members for whom email addresses are held.

Section 67 (1998)

Section Representative:
Julia Collis (Bleasdale)

No news returned this year

Section 66 (1997)

Section Representative:
Katie Mason (Eves)

No news returned this year

Section 65 (1996)

Section Representative:
Catherine Hirons (Charlton)

No news returned this year

Section 64 (1995)

Section Representative:
Emma Lloyd-Williams (Leek)

No news returned this year

Section 63 (1994)

Section Representative:
Belle Morton

Bryonie Clarendon (Leask) Homeschooling has been interesting, attempting to teach three very reluctant boys, so very pleased they are now back at school. Events have been quiet but now with more positive news ahead, we are looking at a busy 2022 with lots of weddings and sporting events.

Jessica Godesen Living in Farnham, daughter is now four and in Reception. Did lose all my work due to Covid but happily have just secured a nice, juicy nine-month contract working for a local marketing agency, so things are looking up again. Also doing a master's in personalised nutrition.

Nancy Lawson (White) Just before the first lockdown we managed to let our house out. We have moved house three times in the last year! It has been an adventure at times, hard, but mostly fun. I have learnt to drive a lorry, done an online nutrition course, and realised it is never too late to change career!

Jemima Mann World events have curtailed my normal tearing about the globe and prevented my considerable contribution to climate change. I am still getting accustomed to attempting to be a useful member of society, (not something that comes naturally), and trying not to throttle my nieces and nephew while assisting in ruining their education.

It has been a phenomenal year for socialising, and I now feel I have the conversational ability of a rabid dog. I am unsure whether I will suffer from verbal diarrhoea or find a corner of the room to stare morbidly out at people, unable to hold a conversation having become a hermit, at the first party I attend after lockdown.

I never thought I would say it, but I am looking forward to moving home and starting work again. Fingers crossed we can get going soon in the B&B, it won't be the same business I had before lockdown (business meetings and business B&B guests), possibly yoga retreats, nutrition/cooking courses and outdoor meetings etc. My ideas change every week!

I hope everyone is well, love to catch up when we can. If anyone is passing there is always a bed.

Belle Morton Managed to fit in my usual trip to Asia and Australia at the beginning of last year before trying desperately to get back from Australia mid-March. Still asking myself why I did that! Anyway, I rocked up on **Sharifa**'s doorstep (she lives down the road) and informed her she had lucked out as I had selected her family to be my bubble - naturally she was thrilled! Honestly, I have had a blast and made the most of what we could do.

The time given back to me this year through less travel and commuting has been a positive and I have zero intention of ever sitting in an office five days a week again. I Marie Kondo'd the flat - if anyone asks me what "sparks joy" I will probably throw them out, but hey, my drawers look like Julia Roberts's in *Sleeping with the Enemy* which I'm sure will be valuable in a post lockdown life somehow?!

Sharifa Parker (Taylor) As I'm sure everyone else has been saying/thinking... what was the last year all about? Rewind back to March 2020, the weather was amazing, working from home full-time was a novelty, having the kids at home was pretty fun, then, bam, before you know it, you're drinking two bottles of wine a night and wondering when this will all end. The highlight has been Boris's updates, and then trying to decipher what it was he actually said, and what the new rules mean.

I had aspirations of learning yoga, reading books, learning new skills, but with the aforementioned alcohol consumption none of those happened. But you definitely learn to appreciate the little things. Was great to go on long walks with the family, appreciate friendships and think about all the things you want to do post this hell.

So, not much news. Working in HR, it was a pretty crazy year work-wise. Youngest started a new school, eldest became a teenager - again, wine consumption. Didn't get a divorce so I'd say that was a big win. Looking forward to spending more time with friends and family and detoxing...maybe!

Ruth Penfold (Baker) No real news of any interest to share. Can't wait until this lock down is over and we can see each other!

Section 62 (1993)

Section Representative
Joanna Runcimann

No news returned this year

Section 61 (1992)

Section Representative:
Coquita Mills

Deborah Dawson (Pain) We're all fit and healthy thankfully, despite current circumstances. Still living in Suffolk and working part-time as a legal PA, which I love. My eldest son, Oliver, is now studying for his A Levels and youngest son Jaspar studying GCSEs. Not much to report this year due to Covid. Hope everyone is keeping well!

Claire Galer (Dorman) All well with us here at Peasebrook. Has been one hell of a year, losing my dear mother and going through such a torrid time of it throughout the Covid pandemic and lockdowns. However best foot forward, and we must strive to continue to make Mother proud as she watches over us.

Our youngest, Sienna, is now 13 and enjoying her second year at Westonbirt. Thankfully off to a great start in Year 7 and has already made firm friends for life. The first year was cut short and homeschooling became the norm and then much the same with Year 8! Westonbirt are doing a fabulous job with the homeschooling, we are all so grateful. Hopefully for Year 9 Sienna will get a full year actually at school!

Rupert, my eldest, is at Exeter Uni in his first year studying Law and loving it, even with lockdown. He has made firm friends, life and studies going well.

Grace, my stepdaughter, is a fabulous hairdresser, under lockdown much of this last year, so helping with childcare for keyworkers.

Jack, my stepson, is in his third year working as a qualified vet, completed first year in practice, then was accepted for a medical internship and now stepping into his specialist neurosurgical residency for the next three years. Then we get to call Dr Galer a diplomat! So proud of all four of our beautiful children.

My dear husband continues to run his great equine veterinary hospital, Peasebrook Equine Clinic, with great excellence and has a super team here, doing great work.

Business for me is busy. I am still heavily involved in my equestrian clothing brand Derriere Equestrian, however this is managed and run by my great team now, with my time taken up predominantly with my role as Head of European Sales and Marketing for Saddlery Brands International (an Australian firm based in Perth), covering Bates, Wintec, and Arena Saddle Brands. Ordinarily working life sees me on and off planes as regular transport, however the pandemic has seen me grounded to the home office, with Zoom the norm and getting to spend so much more time with the family, an absolute bonus.

Am still riding and competing (when not in lockdown!) with my Lusitano Gelding, Sentimiento, at medium level dressage, training to the higher levels to get into that tailcoat!

Sending my love to all my dear Westonbirt sisters near and far. Is odd seeing the boys at school on drop off and pickups nowadays!

Cordelia Gover (Harris) Despite these strange times, I've been quite busy growing my property management company and juggling home schooling for Jazzy (12) and Ellie (10). I've managed to stay in contact with quite a few WB's, even if it has been virtually - **Lina**, **Coquita**, **Claire**, **Charlie**, **Rowls**, **Caroline**, **Candy**, **Sam**, **Doobs** and I even managed to see **Mel** when we were in Lymington for a brief break.

Charlotte Haynes (Hunt) It's been an unusual and challenging year for us all. I've been shielding since the start of the first lockdown, staying safe at home, being well looked after by Ben and Felix (17).

I couldn't'have survived without the support of my WB sisters. **Candy, Claire, Corks, Doobs, Lina, Pulley** and **Sam**, and I have stayed in contact via video calls – much hilarity and unusual topics of conversation have kept me going. Hoping to be able to escape soon and catch up with all the hugs I've been missing.

So looking forward to a proper catch-up as soon as we can. Stay safe and well. Love and hugs to everyone, Charlie xxx

Virginia Kelly I am still living in Malvern and still renovating a barn conversion. We've recently had some fun sledging down the Malvern Hills. We have a new puppy who is gorgeous, and I've been kept very busy juggling homeschooling and work. I've been working on various TV drama productions, like *The Pembrokeshire Murders*, which have been interesting.

Lara Masters Well that was the most bizarre year in the world's history ever, and doesn't look to be getting any less weird with the "let's have a vaccine and another vaccine and another vaccine but don't take that one if you're taking that one, but actually it's better to mix and match, but it doesn't work great against this virus, but it's okay we'll soon have a new vaccine for that, so we'll do this all again in a few months" scenario…

Ironically for me, it was one of the busiest years because when the pandemic hit Pineapple Dance Studios went online. And it was my idea. So, of course, I had to put it all together and steer the ship, and the ship keeps getting bigger, bulkier, and more like 20 people's jobs by the week. Lucky for Mum she had me locked inside in isolation with my husband for the past ten months, both working to keep Pineapple relevant (when I was supposed to be on the set of my autobiographical film! Boohoo).

So now we are streaming a massive online timetable, permanently live and interactive from Pineapple Dance Studios, on a professional broadcast kit (no rubbish-quality Zoom classes), including kids classes, beginners' classes, fitness classes and something for everyone, so email me and I will put you and your kids in a class for free - you could do it with your camera off but you will soon be inspired, and so will your kids. Download Pineapple Live app and get #DancingThroughTheTiers.

I hope you all had a little more restful time, more quality time with the family et cetera, and got some sort of silver lining out of the madness.

Coquita Mills (Marsh) It took a little adjusting to everyone always being at home, and I have a much greater appreciation for all that schools do for all children. It has been wonderful and trying in equal measures, but Barnaby (11) and Cecily (7) continue grow well. We (like Virginia) added a puppy into the mix, which has been so much fun for us all.

Alice Townsend My news is that I am at home, along with everyone else! Homeschooling my two boys, Toby (6) and Mikey (4) has been hard but (sometimes) fun. We have reenacted the Battle of Hastings on the trampoline and made a computer game with an obstacle course around the garden, including having to climb up or jump to grab foil stars hanging from the trees on the way round. We have tracked T-Rex footprints in the snow and made proper treasure maps with properly aged paper (where you crumple it up and flatten it out then dip it in coffee and then, if you feel really brave/foolhardy, burn the edges. Have to confess we did lose a couple of pieces that way and set off the fire alarm once or twice!) But, we have also had our tantrums and tears, lack of motivation, and they do miss their friends. We have the normal problems with logins, internet connection dropping out, and complete confusion over how to teach what presumably is really simple maths at their age!

Away from here, I am still heavily involved with various projects in Ghana and usually go back every October to visit them. Obviously, that was not possible last October and so that is all on a bit of a backburner for now, although I am pleased to say that the rural areas have been largely untouched by Covid (so far). Kwame, my friend writes, "The biggest challenge for us now is the issue of vaccination. Many people are claiming that safety is not assured and serious advocacy against its usage is everywhere in Ghana. The government however is planning to get some by April. Well, when we get there, we will see how we get over it."

My dad still lives on the farm, but on his own after my mother died back in 2014. He has taken lockdown in his stride, using it as a great excuse to avoid having screaming grandchildren trash his house. He plays online bridge three times per week and has been listening to every opera ever performed at the Royal Opera House - nuts!

So, all well here, although it is all getting very boring... enough already! Hope everyone else is OK.

Caroline Walker What a year! As you know, I'm a child and adolescent psychotherapist and have recently started my own business on the farm integrating the horses and nature into my trauma-focused work. Surprisingly, my business initially took a turn for the worse at the beginning of lockdown last March 2020 due to people losing their jobs or being put on furlough and understandably being worried about their income. However, as the year progressed the clients have started to increase and I am now at maximum capacity and I believe I will be for some time now. I am glad that I have the horses and nature in my life so that I can keep myself as healthy as I can so I can be there for my clients. I have seen my 'at-risk' clients face-to-face all the way through lockdown, so it has been quite stressful but a much-needed exercise. I have now had my vaccine so hopefully that will help.

I have had regular online chats with the WB crew (**Charlie Haynes, Corks Gover, Claire Galer, Caroline Wilson, Sam Neary, Deborah Dereham, Candy Morgan**) which has definitely saved my sanity, and we organised our traditional "All Nighter Hogmanay" party on Zoom which was quite fun, although hopefully next time it will be face-to-face!

Caroline Wilson (Pullin) Feel very lucky to have (so far) avoided direct Covid sadness. We have felt very fortunate to live on a farm and tuck ourselves away from society and people safely, yet have so much space around us. Homeschooling has been one of the biggest challenges of all - but it's amazing that during the third lockdown homeschooling has been better than during the first lockdown; the boys are just that bit older and it's made a whole lot of difference, coupled with the poor weather making being indoors much more enjoyable than it was last summer! Oldest now at senior school, youngest at my old prep school, Beachborough, which is a joy to visit daily when not in lockdown!

Just before Christmas HS2 took possession of 100 acres of our farm to commence building. Currently we have the archaeology investigations going on. It's been devastating to the family to watch their farm be ripped up for a train that has questionable benefits; sadly, we have many, many years of misery ahead.

First lambs arrived this week, so about to start lambing once again.

Keep in touch with **Melaine** and **Lina** mainly -but have caught up a bit in video chat with **Charlie, Sam, Corks, Candy** and **Doobs** in New Zealand. This week **Doobs** made us all feel even sadder about lockdown, as where she was the sun was shining and they can do what they want - go to the beach, restaurants, lunches etc. Only thing they are not allowed to do is to leave NZ - how very tough! (UK Feb 2021) Looking forward to when we can say the same!

Section 60 (1991)

Section Representative:
Rebecca Willows

Vanessa Galloway (Konig) wrote to say that she has moved house. She has driven passed Westonbirt quite a bit in the last year and has many fond memories there, especially of the lake, She is pleased that is has been restored. She also wrote that her mother, **Mrs Caroline Konig (Boswell)** passed away in 2018.

Section 59 (1990)

Section Representative:
Julia Roberts (Stubblefield)

No news returned this year

Section 58 (1989)

Section Representative:
Natasha McLeod (Marsh)

No news returned this year

Section 57 (1988)

Section Representative:
Fiona Stokes (Tobin) - (Section 45)

Amanda Spring wrote in February: "I have had a difficult last month. I am in the UK looking after my mother who has had pneumonia. It was a very serious situation, but thankfully she is on the mend. Other than this the last year has not been bad, and I am thankful that Covid has not been so widespread in Poland as in the UK. Horses and dogs are fine, and they very much like the situation that I have been mainly working from home for the last year. Business is difficult, but still moving in the right direction, so we are lucky with that. Not much more to add really, other than I do hope that everyone is keeping well and positive, and that we must hope for easier months and years ahead!"

Jenny Watson (Stubbs) and I have exchanged messages and she is still living in County Cork.

Section 56 (1987)

Section Representative:
Fiona Stokes (Tobin) - (Section 45)

There was a reunion held in Ham Yard, London in December 2019 to celebrate the birthdays of schoolfriends turning fifty (clearly I am somewhat older than them!) I failed to collect any news in 2020 due to the start of the Covid pandemic and a sudden splurge of activity in a volunteer role helping our local Good Neighbour organisation. So, this is an attempt to reconnect with the section!

Arabella Bishop What a strange year. We lost my stepfather in April (not to Covid) and I am up and down to the countryside to look after my mother now. Luckily my sister is here too. My Covid life has made me realize how lucky I am to live by the beach in Dublin – it has become my haven and I tend to head off in the early morning before sunrise to avoid everyone. Brexit is causing me headaches for work – Ireland has an additional import duty of 13.5 per cent on point of entry on all art and antiques. *(Arabella works for Sotheby's FT)* So I am lobbying the government at the moment. I believe M&S shelves are empty here too! Hopefully it will all settle down.

Georgina Busch (Bryon) *(Replied to my email that she is still living in Sweden (Djursholm). She said she would send an update, which hasn't arrived yet.)*

Hetty Clark (Bowden) and I spoke on the phone. She reports she had been having a "lovely lockdown" with all her children at home. Her son Charlie is at Durham University, and his brother Angus is at Cardiff. Daughter Poppy is in Lower Sixth at Cheltenham Ladies, and youngest child, Orlando is in his second year at Radley. Hetty was my informant about the 2019 reunion. She is good friends with **Mary Rennison (Scott)**. I asked her who else she remembers being at the reunion and the mentioned **Georgina Busch (Bryon), Susannah Newell, Juliana Nash (Blanch), Annabel Stafford, Sophie Corr (Hartnell)** and **Lara Webb (Haines)**.

Victoria Calder married Neil Bastin in 2017 but I am not sure if she has changed her name. She writes: "I have had a mixed lockdown of shielding but am able to teach online (and loving live lessons with Year 6) but frustrated by the difference between Seniors who will not speak and Juniors who won't stop! My husband is working from home and is now installed in an upstairs mancave."

Helen Curtis (Senior Stern) runs The Jolly Huntsman pub at Kington St Michael. *(Some years ago, I called in with* ***Sarah Clunie (Roberts)*** *after a Section 53 and 54 reunion at Westonbirt, and we were warmly welcomed, despite never having previously met. On another occasion my husband and I stayed the night at the pub after a local wedding. Again, a warm welcome and great breakfast! FS).*
Helen writes: "After the stop/start we had last year, and the added difficulties of complying with government guidelines, we eventually opened again in July 2020 with all the social distancing and safety measures in place and the new opening hours. When the second lockdown landed, we did not open again after this and we remain closed for the time being *(written in late February)*. We made the right decision between the second and third lockdowns as this meant that we did not have to dispose of stock for the third time running – a mind-blowing and very soul-destroying task of spending hours cataloguing and disposing of beer and lager, not to mention stock from the kitchen. Our preparations for New Year's Eve would have been well in hand by then, and these too would have been futile.

Having not had the opportunity to lead a normal life for the past 17 years since coming here, we have embraced the peace and quiet, although living in a pub that is not open does have its challenges, as everything is geared to commercial use and cooking etc becomes quite a mammoth task. Thankfully, my husband is a vegetarian who would happily live on macaroni cheese, so my culinary talents are not overstretched!

We have just celebrated our fifteenth wedding anniversary. It was nice not to have to work but we could not make the most of it and go out, as everywhere was obviously closed! For now, we sit tight and wait until we can welcome back our lovely customers."

Sarah Harris-Burland (Pilling) reported a slightly different take on life in the Isle of Man during the pandemic. She replied: "We were in lockdown for three-and-a-half weeks which finished on 1st February 2021. We can meet up, go to restaurants/pubs and visit each other in our homes and there is no need to wear masks. The kids were at home for the lockdown. Natasha is in Year 11 (GCSE year) and the uncertainty about assessments or doing exams has been very unsettling. Alexander is in Year 8 so it has been business as usual for him. Looking to spend this year on the island and improve the garden, my big project this year." *(Since that information in late February there was a major spike on the island with subsequent fatalities during March. FS).*

Caitlin Limmer (Gardner) is still living in Isleworth. I left a phone message with her husband but haven't heard any further news.

Libby Warner (Glen) commented from South Australia: "The 2020 bushfires were horrendous and then we had flooding. Our plans to move have not happened yet but just when I think we have emptied the house of 13 years of clutter, another mound surprises me. It gives me the chance to remember and reflect though, so it is not all bad. I am just about to start a new postgraduate certificate at uni for TESOL (teaching English to speakers of other languages) and then another one for Wellbeing and Resilience.

Elder daughter is a social worker. Her husband is committed to adopting as many pugs as possible but thankfully she has stopped him at number two! Their wedding in July 2019 was lovely - unconventional in that her priority was a chocolate fountain for dessert at a restaurant called Concubines, and personal in that her friend made cake toppers that were a Mr & Mrs Pug. It was completely them. A few hours later they held a buffet at their house for just 16 guests. It was perfect except for the Sophie-sized hole in the middle.

We are honoured to be invited annually to Sophie's former school for the presentation of a drama award in her name. We have usually held an annual charitable walk – recently Make A Wish Foundation – but Covid restrictions have stopped that for the moment. Instead, I have spent the time sewing hearts for the 10,000 Hearts project.

Husband is just months from retirement age and is ridiculously excited though I am not sure why. He cannot possibly spoil our dogs any more than he already does. I suspect he is looking forward to playing more golf and reading his Charles Dickens books. Our cruise for our 25th anniversary on the *Queen Elizabeth* was special and marvellous. For those who have yet to enjoy a cruise, do try it when Covid lifts.

In February whilst walking our dogs, we found a pod of five to seven dolphins swimming happily about fifty metres from the beach. It was magical to see these graceful and playful beauties. Between May and September Victor Harbour is along the migratory route of whales, so we shall go down to Middleton which has one of the best lookout spots."

Editor's note re Sections 55 and 55a.

A little confusion arose over the Section numbers for 55 and 55a, and who represents them. Section 55a's rep was unable to gather news this year, and sadly the confusion around Section 55 wasn't sorted out in time for news to be gathered. I fear this is mostly my fault, so many apologies. Below are the names we have associated with the two Sections, we hope all is well, and we fully expect you all to be contacted for contributions to next year's Association News.

Section 55 (1986)

Section Representative:
Emma Lack (Fitch)

Names associated: **Emma Lack (Fitch), Helen Dugdale, Jenny Stubbs, Anabel Whittaker, Fiona Beath, Sally Upton, Patricia Hooper Emma Smith, Paola Rendon, Theresa Cripps, Michelle Crane, Rachel Cairns, Louisa Griffiths, Sophie Rant, Sarah Gladdish, Jo Lucena, Lucy Gay, Tania Hampson, Saskia Salter, Alex Fergusson, Amanda Spring, Annabel Stafford, Cat Bonthrone, Claire O'Gorman, Courtney Chrysslor, Emma Snowdon, Clare Croker, Kate Selby Rickards, Lindsay Upton, Louise Matley, Mari-Ann Kucharek, Naomi Laurence, Penny Samuel, Rebecca Jasper, Victoria Fergusson, Pippa Kidson Trigg, Rachel Smithson, Sarah Fitch, Tara Byng, Caroline Boote**

Section 55a (1982)

Section Representative:
Ouvrielle Roberts (Holmes)

Names associated: **Claire Coode (McCorquodale), Jude Reid, Ouvrielle Roberts (Holmes)** and **Rebecca Whiteoak (Green).**

Sections 53 and 54 (1983-5)

Section Representative:
Sarah Clunie

No news returned this year

Section 52 (1982)

Section Representative:
Lizzie Mobbs (Overton)

Lizzie Mobbs (Overton) What an extraordinary year we have had! 2020 will go down in history for many years to come I fear, as being the root cause for anything bad or that has failed. What have we all learnt this past year? Well I suppose *carpe diem* for starters. We have, as a family, managed to keep going and make the most of being together, through pretty much all of the first two lockdowns and like everyone else learnt to adjust and appreciate what we have within our own square mile. So my news this past year, I imagine, will be reflective of all of yours.

Way back in May, I volunteered for Salute the NHS and helped to deliver a million meals to frontline workers, and then in August we welcomed a new addition to the family - our first grandchild!

Section 51 (1981)

Section Representative:
Lizzie Mobbs (Overton)

Diana Davidson I was invited to become a Fellow of the Energy Institute, relatively recently. One of only eighty women in the world to have achieved the highest level of membership, in recognition for making a difference in the clean tech and renewable energy industry.

Section 50 (1980)

Section Representative:
Antonia Doggart

Thank you to you all for writing in. I've enjoyed catching up with you and I am glad you have managed to get through the past year relatively unscathed. I always enjoy reading what you have been doing in recent years as I have happy memories of some of the hilarious times we all had at school!

Paula Blatcher I live in Florida and have been here since 1982 when my dad moved here with his new wife. It was definitely a big cultural change in so many ways from what I was used to in the Caribbean (I had been at boarding school in Barbados) and the UK. I won't deny it is really pleasant to be in the warm weather and sometimes it can get a bit too hot, but we manage, as we all have air conditioning, so it is bearable.

My husband and I got the virus starting Christmas Day and it was not a pleasant experience; we have recovered, however, and are very grateful for that. We managed to treat ourselves holistically and happily we got through without any major complications. (I'm a holistic health coach and practitioner and work with clients around the world, including via Zoom.)

We did plan on going to the UK this past summer but due to the pandemic had to cancel our plans. It was disappointing, as I was taking my two youngest sons (grown men actually) to show them around, including Westonbirt and the continent. We had a nice trip planned but all got squashed, and now I'm not sure when we will be able to go. It would be nice to see everyone one day!

Claire Catterall Claire continues in her role as Senior Curator at Somerset House in London and is currently working on a big exhibition about the *Beano*, due to open in October 2021. She works from home these days, which is a black barn with a red roof in Kent, shared with her husband Matt and two miniature dachsies, Pip and Pongo. She says it's definitely quieter since son Solomon moved to uni (Queen Mary University of London) to study Cultural History (like mother, like son!).

Antonia Doggart (Ross) In the middle of March 2020 we returned from our happy Kenyan coastal family holiday to find Clare's boyfriend ill with Covid. Fortunately, he recovered from the resultant pneumonia, and Clare somehow managed to nurse him and keep her events company running, by doing deliveries, cooking hundreds of meals for the NHS and catering for photo shoots and now it's exciting and all-go again with the brides! Charlie had to leave his field guide and wildlife protection job in the fever tree forests of Limpopo because of lockdown in South Africa. He's now a teaching assistant in a London prep school. James passed out from Sandhurst in April to join the Light Dragoons.

I spent most of the past year supporting family, helping my mother to care for my stepfather, and a handful of close friends and neighbours – all of whom died from cancer.

In November I decided to embark on cold-water swimming at my local beach but on the first swim had transient global amnesia – and all because I forgot the golden rules of how to enter the water properly! A warning to us all to be careful. I'll stick with tennis, walking my dog Monty, yoga and breathwork.

When it's been possible, I have enjoyed helping with a local arts and crafts group and with the youth education charity, Arundel Castle Cricket Foundation, and trying to prevent yet more housing development at the Witterings! It's been good to see **Lou** and **Rose** this year, as well as **Tanya** in the US and **Pippa** in Canada, all via WhatsApp.

Sarah Frost I am living in Amberley with my husband and dog. This is what I have been up to all this time:

After Westonbirt I went to The Royal Agricultural College and was one of the first girls there. I went on to work in the Farms Department for Smith-Woolley overseeing Highgrove and the Duchy farms. I went on to work for Wafic Said at Tusmore for 20 years: we built a Palladian mansion which I ran. I then came back to Gloucestershire and worked for the Beaufort Polo Club, then got involved in charity work. I am on the committees for Tetbury Hospital and the Nelson Trust. I was head of fundraising for the Cotswolds Dogs and Cats Home and raised the funds to build a brand new multi- million-pound centre. I then decided to set up my lifestyle business and lost all my regular clients when Covid hit. I also hadn't been trading long enough to get Government support, so double whammy!

Lalage Gittoes (Wood) I have been living in New Zealand for the past 17 years. We emigrated here in December 2003 - we being my husband Will, and our three children who are now adults. I have worked for the Pacific Leprosy Foundation for the past 14 years as a fundraiser and jack-of-all-trades and we live about 50 km from Christchurch in the South Island. We built (or rather had built for us) a house on ten acres - called a "lifestyle block" over here - and we have horses, chickens, and dogs. I have always been lucky enough to work some of the time from home, but thanks to

Covid I now work four days a week from home and just touch base in the office one day a week. I have been so lucky to have a better lifestyle thanks to Covid - something that is far from the case for most people.

Tanya Hart (Gee) After 16 years living in Chicago, in 2014 we decided to sell the house and move to Seattle, Washington. We had a good run in Chicago, opened three wine shops over eight years, and a restaurant. We felt it was time to move back to the west coast, to be closer to my aging dad and our friends here.

Gabby, now 23, graduated from high school in Seattle and was offered a spot to play soccer at the University of Redlands. She graduated from Redlands in the middle of pandemic 2020 and is currently living with us at home, while doing her master's in Terrorism and Homeland Security online, at the American University in DC. She hopes to be in DC this August for her final term, graduating in December. She intends to work in intelligence for one of the government agencies or to go into the military.

Harry is 20, graduated from Army and Navy Academy high school in 2019, where his senior/final year he tore not one but two anterior cruciate ligaments playing football (American). Undeterred by the universities that dropped his recruitment offers, he came home, worked hard, recovered brilliantly, and is currently living in Mission Viejo, California, playing football for a small junior college. He is hoping next season to be recruited by a big Division 1 school, to play and finish out university. He is studying Engineering. Shep played football in college, so we are all a bit sporty in our household.

Shep and I celebrated our 27th wedding anniversay last October. We are so close to being empty nesters, but are loving having the kids home while we can. Shep is a packaging engineer for Westrock Packaging, and his main account is Amazon, so has been very fortunate to be busy during the pandemic. We have all had to adjust, like most people, to a family working out of the 'home office'. The pandemic brought lots of new normals, and despite consuming too much food, too much alcohol and adopting a five-month-old American Staffordshire pup we named Augie (who is now 15 months and 80 lbs), we are very lucky we all get along!

After a very privileged and well travelled 33 year career in the wine industry, I decided to switch career paths completely, and move towards something in 'sustainability'. I started in the hemp industry, which back in 2015/2016 was exploding. I learned a lot about hemp, made some incredible relationships, not the least of which was my business partner David Abecassis. David and I formed Titan Bioplastics in 2017. We spent 2018 working with hemp plastics, but quickly realized the industry simply wasn't ready and didn't have the supply chain.

We turned our attention to what is possible today, with our present technology and 35 years of polymer and biodegredation expertise. Titan Bioplastics was recently named one of four top global companies leading nanotechnology innovation in barrier properties and plastics. We are still a small start up, but growing nicely with some great clients. You can see what we do on our website www.titanbioplastics.com. Personally I'm loving what I do, feel I am contributing in small ways to a healthier planet, and learning enormous amounts about the science, the EU, UN global directives in plastics and circular economy solutions.

We truly enjoy the northwest outdoor lifestyle, and despite some challenging politics of late it's a beautiful place to live. Our house is on a 200ft bluff overlooking the Puget Sound and Olympic Mountains, its our Zen space, and everyday I wake up and know that I am an extremely blessed and fortunate person. Hope all you Westonbirtians are doing well and are healthy and happy. Wishing you all the very best for 2021 and beyond.

Zan Hartley (Jowett) I'm sure we will all have pretty much the same response re our news, after such a bad 12 months.

The good news is I became a granny for the second time, back in October, to Willow, a little sister for Purdy. All a bit traumatic at the time as she was rather poorly, needing major surgery, but I'm pleased to report that the NHS were fantastic, and she is now doing well. As they live nearby, we are very active grandparents!

We can't wait to be able to resume normal life out of lockdown. If anyone is passing Harrogate, it would be lovely to have visitors once more.

Jane John (Thomas) I really have no news of any consequence. My son's wedding was postponed from last year so now we are hopeful it may take place this August. We are just about to embark on a house extension just as everyone else is thinking of downsizing! I honestly think it is lockdown-itus! We also have a new black lab puppy who is keeping me active.

I am still involved with the Lord's Taverners but obviously we have been unable to do any fundraising - ironically our last event was St David's Day 2020! I do hope we can have a get-together soon. 40 years is MAD! Where did that time go?! I love seeing everyone via Facebook - it is a great way of staying in touch.

Rose Lucas No news but I'm really grateful to everyone who helped me to apply for new O Level certificates (at vast expense). Lesson to everyone: never lose your school certificates!

Kate Marchbank The poor old UK has had a rough time. We meantime are stuck in Australia. It's very hard to get an exemption to get out. No other democracy in the world (except NZ I think) has done this. We are on a par with North Korea! Anyway, we have been mercifully less impacted - although of course no country has escaped the impact of the dreaded virus. Ironically between Simon and me, we have six children and five of them are in the UK, so it is a bit sad we haven't been able to get to see them all.

Anyway, no real news but we live partly in Sydney (NSW) and partly in Noosa, Queensland. I am newly retired and love to swim still - Simon is partly tied up in Board work but leaves much time for travel (although this hasn't happened this year). We are hoping to get across to the UK in October once Australia opens its borders and vaccination has been done.

Astrid Mitchel (Sadler) The main event of the past year is that I became a grandmother. Eldest son Tom and Kim got married up at Blair Atholl in late November 2019 and Isobel arrived almost exactly a year later. I was able to go up and spend time with them all (they live just north of Edinburgh) shortly after her birth, but then back came lockdown so that was it thereafter.

However, Kim and Isobel have been staying for a week as some major work was needed on their house, and it was lovely to have them. Isobel is now four months so is at that great stage of being a proper little person without actually moving about.

Other son Rory is down in London working for the Foreign Office. He managed to get home for Christmas, and also last summer, but other than that we haven't seen him.

Work has been somewhat challenging – I was already working from home, so no change there, but a large part of our business is international conferences, which have gone out of the window. We are managing to stay afloat by streamlining the business and building up publishing and consultancy but crossing our fingers that travel will resume in the next six to nine months and we can start getting back to normal. On the plus side, the constant travel was getting harder and harder, and it's been great not having to set foot on a plane this past year.

Other than that, life on the farm continues as usual and this last year the benefits of living out in the middle of nowhere with plenty of space and freedom have really come into their own. And I have also had the time to get into some serious gardening (with limited success), take up cycling to get fit (ditto), and do some much-needed renovation on the house, including replacing the 40-year-old kitchen (a work in progress… I am sitting in a building site as I type, but it's proving more successful than the gardening or fitness regime).

Kate Morris I am working on a collection of short stories, while completing an MA in Creative and Life Writing at Goldsmiths College. I work part time for the British Red Cross, which was particularly busy during the first lockdown, and a friend and I have started an Instagram account www.instagram.com/dog_diary_london in which we do on-the-spot interviews with dog owners, walking their dogs.

Sally Reeve (Bartlett) I'm still living in Wallingford, Oxfordshire, with my husband, and am lucky to have both daughters living nearby and our son is not too far away in London.

My elder daughter is married, and we have a lovely, lively three-year-old granddaughter who we see often and feel very lucky that we have been able to continue this through the last two lockdowns as part of a childcare bubble.

My work as a remedial massage therapist has been somewhat disrupted on and off over the last year due to the pandemic. However, I have managed to find plenty to do with walks, decorating, gardening, and doing jigsaw puzzles, as well as researching my family tree. Not sure I want to go back to work!

As a retired nurse I have applied to help with the vaccination programme - a very protracted process. I have been accepted now but awaiting further instruction as to when and where they might find a use for me!

Not very much else to add, but I am feeling grateful to have weathered the storm relatively unscathed so far and I'm really hoping, as we all are, that life will return to some normality soon.

Jane Roikenen (Archer) No news from my side but I'm still in Portugal, still building my house, looking after my mum as my dad died last year, and life drifts by - although I am considering starting a small business over here so that I actually have to leave my "happy chair" (my swinging chair that catches the sun in winter and the shade/breeze in summer).

Cherry Stratford (Perkins) No great news from me – I am still the Bursar of a small independent school in Pembrokeshire, but we are expanding all the time and are opening a sixth form in September.

We have survived the pandemic unscathed - no illness and work has continued pretty much as normal for both my husband and me. I see some updates on Facebook - **Juliet, Tanya, Phillipa, Lois, Lou** and although I rarely post anything, it's nice to see theirs!

Cathy Street (Dyer) I continue to work in mental health research with Warwick Medical School, obviously at some distance. Christmas and New Year were "interesting" in that my household all went down with Covid, each of us having totally different symptoms. Not a nice experience, I have never felt such fatigue. Thankfully, we are all fully recovered save for my palate, which is still odd and I have gone completely off coffee! I hope this finds everyone well.

Juliet Tomlinson I've had no concerts for over a year now, but I've been teaching cello on Zoom and clearing my parents' house. We're lucky to live in a lovely rural setting on Mayhill in Gloucestershire and everything was delivered to us, so the horrible pandemic has felt rather remote in some ways. We have been extremely fortunate.

I've also been doing lots of work with my three horses. One is a star at agility and keeps winning competitions, much to my amazement. I'm also bringing on a beautiful young Haflinger horse and I hope that he will become my next horse archery steed! I qualified as a horse archer in 2019 and so I could be in the next Robin Hood movie. **Kate Wood** was amazing and helped me wash my grey mare before a competition. I also see **Catherine Murray** very regularly.

My daughter, Jess, got married in September of 2020 and she and her lovely Scottish husband have just moved into their first house in Walthamstow. She is a trainee solicitor and a triathlete, and he is an actuary. Funnily enough, they are both very musical and sing together in church choirs in London.

Georgina Turner I have been occupied with various, though a focussed few, addictions since we last met - motherhood, art, culture, entrepreneurialism, and increasingly politics. It has been neither a pilgrim's nor a rake's progress.

Lavinia Unwin I feel as though I have had rather a lazy year with very little work, but I did manage to cater for a fantastic lady's 90th birthday in August. Still, I think it will be all systems go once we finally get the green light and there will be plenty of parties, so I can come back refreshed. Sometimes a break from routine is a good thing.

My parents are both in their eighties and although unaffected by Covid, are needing more "supervision" - they don't ask for help, but a few casseroles and cakes go down well! I have two stray cats that were living rough outside but have now become total lounge-lizards - it has been good to have some extra time to give them.

Apart from that I have been keeping up with friends and family and like everyone else watching too much Netflix. I can't wait to be able to see people and just do simple things like having supper with friends. It's got to the point where meeting someone new on a dog walk and putting the world to rights is often the highlight of my day. Roll on the vaccine - I see some of our year group have had their first jab, so I'm hoping mine will be soon.

Lou Walker (Foord) Hello all. Funny old year – I hope you've all got through ok so far and can see the light at the end of the tunnel. I know I'm not the first to say it but am so thankful we live in the middle of nowhere with a garden and glorious countryside. I would probably have been a wreck if I'd been locked down in a city.

I've been very busy, learning how to be a YouTuber (the benefits of having a daughter and her boyfriend at home a lot last year), running weight loss, health and wellbeing courses and building my health coaching practice - all possible thanks to Zoom. I've also had another research article published, this time in *BMJ Nutrition, Prevention & Health* - something I'm really chuffed about, particularly as a non-academic. It's all focused on weight loss and improved metabolic and mental health, using diet and lifestyle changes. The "diet" involved is becoming more accepted - a low carb approach - but I often prefer to call it a low carb "real food" approach. Having worked and written around this for about eight years now (often being thought of as a bit of a nutter), it's exciting to be involved in several projects helping it to become mainstream. 2021 will be an exciting year on that front! It will help tackle so many increasingly common conditions which were incredibly rare 40 years ago before we were all told to avoid fat! Ways to help us all improve our health and immunity are so important, aren't they? I think more people - even Boris perhaps - are realising that now. Long way to go! If you're interested in any of this, do have a look at my website: *www.louwalker.com*.

My family are all ok. Jack's teaching science, specialising in physics, in Leeds. His girlfriend is just qualifying as a doctor and they seem to be pretty settled in Yorkshire for the next couple of years at least. Charlie is still dying to perform more but she's meanwhile flourishing in a tech firm in Bristol. Husband Simon is still paramotor king, heading up a company that makes what he calls "back-pack aircraft".

It's been great to see **Tonia** a few times. Sadly, she lives too far away for us to have met up much last year. Fingers crossed for this year, though!

Kay Walton (Gardner) At the risk of repeating what so many others have said, it's been a strange year. None of the social markers we'd got used to happened and we've been reduced to getting excited by haircuts and supermarket outings - or not, as the case may be. My husband and one of my sons have been working from home since the first lockdown, meaning our food bill has increased exponentially, whilst our other son and his girlfriend were driven to start living together by the first lockdown, which has been the making of their relationship - we're delighted to see it. I haven't really kept in touch with other WB girls apart, of course, from my sister, **Philippa**, and I know she meets up with **Jane John (Thomas)** now and again in Cardiff.

Kate Wood (Oura) 2020 started well with a lovely skiing holiday in Switzerland and then lockdown arrived. I am lucky to live on the edge of Minchinhampton Common and love my garden, so life was not too difficult, especially as I retired from veterinary work in 2018. The biggest headache was having to share my house full time with my husband! I decided to learn Italian with Duolingo and have continued with that.

My daughter was getting married in early June 2021, so this has been postponed to April 2022.

I have volunteered with the St John Ambulance to be a Covid vaccinator and had my first dose of the vaccine in February.

I am so looking forward to seeing friends and family when we are allowed.

Section 49 (1979)

Section Representative:
Fiona Merritt

Funso Adegbola (Ige) I am thankful that we all made it, and are still making it, through the global pandemic. My school, The Vale College, now 27 years old, had to pivot from on-site learning to remote learning for six months last year. We resumed in-class learning in September, observing all the Covid protocols. The students were eager to return to classes with their friends, but they couldn't hug and be physically close, which they missed, especially on the football field and netball court. Hopefully, by September, when we all have been vaccinated, we can resume school as usual, playing games and sports together.

On a personal note, my daughter got married at a small ceremony in April 2021. I became a grandmother first in October 2019 when my son had a baby daughter, followed by a son in March 2021. I am thoroughly enjoying my new status as a Nana of two! Absolutely thankful to God for His grace and favour.

Mary Ashworth (Moriarty) Gosh, what a time it has been! Since lockdowns began we have had a fourth grandchild, Isaac, sold a house, and our youngest daughter Rachel has got married and finally left home. Who could have imagined such a thing as a Zoom wedding? It was actually a really enjoyable experience - just six there in person, but many more on Zoom including the groom's family in Singapore! So, we await the wedding reception planned for July and then the Singapore wedding party, hopefully in 2022! We still have a houseful - including two lovely grandchildren who keep us on our toes. Ruth is homeschooling (had planned to anyway) and we are all learning lots of new things!

Rob and I spent quite a bit of the various lockdowns stranded in Devon, which had its pros and cons. I found myself shopping there for the family of some shielding old WBs! Rob had already set in motion a change in his work life, so it all slotted together quite well with the enforced working from home, and we now work for a few churches and charities including a foodbank in Yorkshire which has grown considerably in the pandemic situation. We have mostly been in pretty good health through it all, including my mum, now 92.

Cheng Sim Chan This year we've mostly been sheltering in place at home with my expeditions comprised of going to work, pharmacies and supermarkets - very unexciting! We've had a number of people passing away last year and this, mostly from illness and not related to Covid. Trying to deal with friend's parental/spousal loss with contact restrictions in place was a challenge. I had hoped the new Chinese Year of the Ox would be the beginning of better things but not so far – fingers crossed still though, for us all.

Neelam Christie (Gunther) It has been a really strange year especially in GP land. It is amazing how quickly IT can be developed when there is a crisis. I think some people actually thought we were doing less work when in fact we were overwhelmed with calls so last year we worked through Easter and May bank holidays. Throughout we have been calling the vulnerable and offering reassurance that we're still open and providing access and support to the brilliant volunteers who did their shopping and much more. Then there was the setting up of the Covid vaccine centre-incredibly hard work, but we did it - standing in tents, freezing cold during December and February snow. Primary Care Networks (practices all working together) have reached the 70,000 mark for jabs in Barnet and rising.

Family-wise, it has been hard with hospital admission for Ma during the first lockdown and husband Jon had surgery during second lockdown. Pleased to report that all are now well and double jabbed, including Marcelle, my younger sister.

Seonaid Coreth (Goodbody) Still keeping busy and thankful family and friends doing well so far. Looking forward to when social distancing is a dim memory, and to our first dressage mini-event for 18 months in mid-May.

Myfanwy Edwards (Lougher) To say the past 12 months have been very difficult would be an unnecessary understatement! However, I am extremely privileged to live in the most beautiful rural setting, with plenty of space around me to walk the dogs etc. Life on the farm continued as normal, with the livestock completely unaware of Covid or the lockdown!

One positive out of the pandemic and last April's shortages in the supermarkets was people's reconnection to their local area and to where their food comes from. I have been involved in the Farmers' Market for the past 20 years and set up an online version, the Cowbridge Food Collective, four years ago; both were bumping along quietly, not setting the world alight. We had to adapt very quickly to new rules and regulations to keep both our producers and customers safe but have enjoyed a significant increase in sales and new shoppers. It has been an extremely busy year preparing food for the Collective every Thursday and the Farmers' Market every Saturday, but a joy to supply people with good locally produced food and to hear the positive feedback about our products. Although it has quietened down a little recently, we continue to thrive, and I hope that everyone remembers who fed them when they were struggling and continue to shop locally. If any Westonbirt old girls ever find themselves in Cowbridge, South Wales, do pop into the Farmers' Market on Saturday morning and say hello!

We welcomed a new granddaughter during lockdown at the end of March 2020, who, despite not being able to meet others or socialise, other than with her sister, is a delightful, outgoing little girl. That brings our grandchild count to four. The eldest of our four grandchildren should have been doing his GCSEs this year; both he and his sister have had a very disrupted academic year but have been invaluable helping on the farm and I am sure have received many great life lessons despite missing out on school!

I fear it will be some time yet before we are able to visit our eldest son in Australia, but thank goodness for technology - we have at least been able to talk regularly, and to see him, even if only on a screen.

Janet Forbes Glad to be able to report that I eventually recovered from the gorilla virus and have managed to avoid coronavirus. Kenya locked down very quickly and concentrated on isolating any outbreaks. There is still an overnight curfew, restricted opening hours, work at home policy, where possible, and the vaccination rollout will take many months to complete; but there does seem to be some light at the end of the tunnel.. No break in the work levels for me though, which is reassuring on one level but does feel like I am often welded to my computer and desk. Like last year, I am not risking planning a big trip until the world is more settled, but, fingers crossed, my god-daughter and her parents be able to visit me for Christmas 2021, as planned.

Alison Kerby (Wilson) It has been a very strange year for us all and I hope that everyone has kept safe and well. The family are all carrying on as best as they can and thankfully have managed to avoid Covid. My daughter, Georgie and her boyfriend moved out of London a few weeks ago and are staying with us pending buying a house in Bristol. Olly is now an Army Officer and living in Colchester and Fraser is still farming at home, breeding sheep and calf rearing amongst other activities.

Work for us stopped for a few weeks last spring but then restarted, and we have been very busy ever since, which is typical of most of the building industry this year.

Joanna Kidson (Rowson) I almost feel guilty talking about life here, as New Zealand's strategy of "Go Hard, Go Fast" seems to have paid off. As a nation, we spent six weeks from late March 2020 in Level 4 lockdown which saw all of Philip's pending contracts evaporate overnight, leaving him with one small contract servicing analysers, which has continued occupying one day a fortnight since then.

Philip became our nominated shopper, shopping for us, his father, and a number of other friends in the vulnerable category (over 70), which provided him with some opportunities to talk to other people.

I was fortunate that I was able to work from home, turning the spare room into my "office" although I'm surprised to have had my second Financial Year End (31 March for New Zealand) in this setup. From mid-May we have been at Level One (almost business as usual but encouraged to scan into any business we go to) with the occasional stint at Level Two when Covid cases breached border protection. The Government has been very cautious about vaccinating, but Pfizer rollout is now underway with the final Phase 4 due to start in July, after which there may be some thought of our borders opening up again.

Bex had recently started her first job at the Ministry of Education, working on policy for international students – obviously a very interesting and challenging time. Jono's studies at University of Canterbury moved online which he found particularly demanding, so he was relieved when they were able to go back to lectures in the middle of the year. Bex was able to join us for Christmas, and we went to visit Jono in late January. Jono came home for the recent mid-semester break where the three of us enjoyed a fantastic three days out on the lake before the first frost.

I have completed my first full season of sailing Tanifarr, with Philip, for many years, but the only silverware to show for the season will be the Single-Handed Series so I am not sure if I will be asked back! Jono's old room is now my craft room where "re-use" projects include facemasks, cake stands from plates, candles, and gift and bottle bags from curtain samples. As we are currently downsizing Philip's dad from his independent living, one-bedroomed unit into rest-home level care, I'm hoping the planned autumn church fair will assist in clearing the craft room!

Joan Lowton (Mullens) I've been at work for all the last year but was redeployed twice to our community service instead of outpatients, which was a definite change of scene. I've mostly been doing phone and zoom calls, which is very different to normal hands on physio - for some people I've been very pleasantly surprised at how well they have done, so that's good.

No significant travels to report but we are due to head up to a self-contained cottage in the North York Moors, which will be lovely. We have now got a half allotment which, along with book club, the garden, planning and dreaming of travelling, and family Zoom meetings, have kept us more or less sane this last year.

We're hoping to fit in more travel and visiting from August when Andrew retires and I reduce down to three days a week - I don't feel quite ready yet to retire, but this may change when I'm leaving for work and Andrew is still lying in bed!

Philippa Meikle (Main) What I miss(ed) most in lockdown is being able to have friends into the house. Although Scotland didn't have the second national lockdown in the autumn, our relaxation of rules remained stricter throughout the summer and particularly from September onwards. Our rule of six was two households only, and we were unable to socialize in each other's houses from the end of September. We are looking forward to 17th May when we hope to be allowed one other couple inside the house, eight months after we were last allowed to do so.

The third lockdown since Boxing Day has seemed particularly long through the cold winter months. However, we are acutely aware that we are so fortunate compared to a lot of people. We live in a lovely area and have a garden, so benefitted from having more time to spend in it. Our daily walks took us along the river Tay and at the weekends we treated ourselves to a walk in a nearby wood.

We watched the flora and fauna through spring into early summer, the highlights being learning to recognize the call of nuthatches, and watching red squirrels including a family with three babies, which were still thriving by the autumn. My husband worked from home throughout and is still doing so and both our sons likewise in their respective flats.

Fiona Merritt I've kept busy this last year by joining NHS/RVS volunteers (pharmacy/shopping trips on my bicycle helped the exercise quota too) and also due to significant increases in support/care requirements for various family members. So thankful for unlimited phone and internet packages but concerned for "square eyes" with the vast array of online options that proliferated!

Local SC duties were initially stopped with last year's lockdown, to keep us in reserve, but encouraged again from late April.

Most diving plans were rolled over but we did manage reduced numbers of weekends to Porthkerris and Plymouth, with the side benefit of a Torquay visit to see my 94-year-old uncle and his wife before he died in the autumn. Milton Keynes did see snow a few times but never for long and no compensation for a week on the slopes with friends. All trips/visits rather on hold now, but I'm still hoping we all come through as unscathed and as quickly as possible.

Marion Minton I'm going through a bad time just now but hope to be in a position to update with better news.

Paula Palmer (Chin) Glad to report that we have all stayed well, even with enduring a very cold barbecue for six to celebrate my 60th in early December. Rebecca, our elder daughter, has just exchanged contracts nearby and Lauren, our younger daughter, and her partner found jobs and a flat in Leicester last summer. We have bought a small chalet on the southern edge of Snowdonia which will be the focus of our travel plans for a while yet, with the vegetables in our garden keeping us busy when at home.

Andrea Radman (Beattie) Nothing major to report for me but Rachel has completed her master's in Modern Building, so is looking for more relevant employment. I've kept up my own yoga but even less teaching this last year as on-line options did not appeal. Like many others, I've been in contact more with elderly parents.

Sally Scheffers The farm, myself and my 91-year-old mother all ticking along still, with Covid/lockdown not changing what the cattle, sheep, chickens, et al require! Luckily we have all stayed safe and well.

Nikki Tehel (Palmer) My indulgence for the first lockdown was a refresher/boot camp for Yoga Teachers by Zoom and I helped out with telephone support calls and grocery deliveries; second lockdown unfortunately memorable for Mum's stroke and death, and third lockdown memorable for Lulu suddenly being unable to walk or wee and having emergency hemilaminectomy surgery from which she is recovering, although still needing to be carried up and down stairs.

I've been volunteering for the jab centre at Brixham Rugby Club recently, and also restarted assessments for PAT (Pets As Therapy), but am currently enjoying a week in Windsor in the back garden pod of friends - a holiday! We took Mum's cousin to lunch (a real lift for her as her first outing), and are due to a barbecue in Windsor Castle grounds with family friends, including one of the four in the choir for Prince Philip's funeral.

Lucy Toyn (Phillips) My main news is that Jonathan and I are now grandparents after Felicia gave birth to Eloise in October, but otherwise we (including Jeremy in Munich, Felicia in Reading, Christopher and Graham in London, and my parents in Taunton) continue as best we can, including my adapting to providing physio over the phone. We are all looking forward to when we can see each other properly again.

Marguerite Williams (Morris) It still seems weird to be in my third career at the age of 60, but IT auditing is proving very interesting and seems to suit my curiosity. It also helps me keep up with the dinner conversation of my software engineering home co-workers (husband, Jock, and son, David). I was recently promoted to manager at work so now I need to learn how to manage people – fortunately, I seem to work with adults, who are supportive and want to be part of a team.

Not having air-conditioning at home proved a bit uncomfortable for a few months in the summer, but we coped. Jock took it upon himself to build desks for myself and David. He sourced beautiful slabs of redwood and American elm, then spent much time sanding and varnishing. We have now moved on to planting the side yard to give my window something to look at other than weeds. We still need to get the rats out of the attic, but I think they are just a permanent fixture.

I'm missing getting back to the UK to visit Helen in Scotland and my mum (**Mrs. Anne Morris**) who is now in a care home, near St Austell in Cornwall, so we make do with video calls for now.

Section 48 (1978)

Section Representative:
Amiel Price

Only a few replies this year, partly because some O Level leavers have now moved to Section 50, but I hope we do better next time.

Johanna Justice Not a lot to report, but so far so good in that my partner and I are still here. Our families are all ok, with my brother and sister-in-law both in the front line, being teachers and looking after the vulnerable and teaching online. Thankfully, the weather in the summer was good so I spent most of it in the garden. Cornwall spent a good deal of time in Tier 1, but has suffered due to inconsiderate people travelling from higher tiers and some unscrupulous holiday home-owners having people to stay in the second lockdown and over New Year.

Compared to other parts of the country we have got off lightly, and my heart goes out to anyone from the Westonbirt alumni who has lost a family member due to this pandemic. I have kept my mind active by doing crosswords and playing Scrabble on the computer every day.

The dog, Rigsby, who is still bouncy at the age of eight, keeps us fit with daily walks, and I am eating more healthily since the beginning of this year.

On Friday nights my partner and I now have games night which also coincides with drinks night, so it starts off amicable and then gets competitive. Life goes on, and if asked, my reply is “ticking along”. So, to everybody, “keep ticking along”, whether it be a fast day or a slow one, see the nature around you, and breathe.

Susan Kennedy (Sheard) I left my job with Restore in February, having lost another friend to cancer, and feeling that the stress of work was not worth the money; I timed my leaving perfectly, with a trip to Cape Town to watch hubby, Gordon Kennedy, playing cricket for the Lords Taverners. He has played for them often and has recently become a trustee. This brilliant charity does so much good for disabled and disadvantaged children in the UK and abroad. We had travelled with little thought of the Covid flu in Wuhan and flew back to London as the toilet roll hoarding had started to be “a thing”.

My potential part-time job disappeared, and our eldest son returned from a trip to South America with his girlfriend and was locked down with us for ten weeks - it was spring/summer so not too bad. I then managed to get a part-time job with an old supplier and am very happily doing website work and social media for a small software company. They’re a good bunch of people and I have adjusted to a much smaller salary - this last year it's been quite easy not to spend money!

Our youngest son is still in Toronto, so we have not seen him for over 18 months - but thank goodness for Zoom. Actor husband, Gordon, has been seen in *Harlots* (mostly clothed thank goodness) and *The Spanish Princess* and is about to go and film an episode of *Grantchester*! He also produces a lot of comedy drama for BBC Radio 4 and is about to record a second series of something called *Alone* which is very funny.

I’m in quite regular contact with **Rachel Dillon (Nobes)**, **Angie Yorath (Haviland)**, **Claire Staveley**, **Tella Wormington**, **Cally Henson**, **Gilly McCollum (Isaac)**, **Fee Rabson (Robertson)**, **Vanessa Reid (Turvill)** and **Nicola Morgan (Spencer)**.

A few of us ex-Holfords were able to meet up for Angie's 60th last February. She was over from Chicago, where she lives, and we were joined by her dear father Edmund Haviland who, well into his 90s, was in his cups to be with all the ‘young' women! Angie’s sister **Maggie Metcalfe (Haviland)** was there too, and we worked out that since **Nicky Spencer** had stayed on in 1978 and had become Head of Holford, there were three Heads of Holford at the table: Maggie, myself, and Nicky!

I managed to fit in two virtual marathons in 2020 - another friend is having treatment for cancer and I raised money for the Christie Hospital. In March I did a mad solo marathon, starting at 5am, and did 42 laps of a local park, which wasn't great for my hip not changing direction, but I recovered in time to take part in the first ever Virtual London Marathon in October - it was the 40th London, and my 20th marathon, so a special day. It did not stop raining and we missed the huge crowds of the London Marathon, but we all enjoyed it and raised lots of money for the hospital.

Roll on spring, summer - some sort of normality? Please? Take care everyone.

Joanna Melhuish (Marchbank) We've been very locked down all year, but I have managed to get to Sydney (with a two-week quarantine and many a change to flights) to visit my parents and sister **Kate (Marchbank)** and Jonathan too. I really wanted to see them - it has been so long and seemed so far away this year. I also visited Tom, my eldest. He is an ICU doctor there and couldn't get permission to leave Australia. I feel incredibly lucky. I left the rest of the family in the UK just for a month - locked down with Simon holding the fort. We have had kids living/working with us for different lockdowns as their own teeny apartments weren't adequate for four flatmates doing their presentations/calls etc. Max's girlfriend is cooking for the NHS/other charities - lots of baking, sourdough, and walks.

Ella and Chris got engaged, so that was such wonderful news for us, and are moving nearer to us in Richmond. The wedding is due in 2022 if allowed!

Mia is at Bath University, which isn't really what it sounds, with Zoom lectures and nothing in reality – "self-teaching" she calls it. She is the only one of four braving the uni house in the second year, and is lonely when her lovely French boyfriend can't be around. Luckily, her third year is in industry (AstraZeneca as a medical research person) in Gothenburg this September. But will that happen?

Amiel Price Our first lockdown started on 23rd March 2020 and with the good weather I spent a lot of time gardening at home and keeping in email contact with the volunteers from Swansea's Botanical Gardens. We tried to keep everyone's spirits up with funny stories, poetry challenges and even a Chelsea bun cooking competition, sending in photos for comparison. Remember those marvellous buns we had during the 11am break in the kitchen courtyard at school?

2020 was the 75th anniversary of VE Day and I found a photo of Mum, **Maureen Price (Craig) Section 17,** flying her flag in the garden on the original VE Day in 1945. It must have been rather poignant as her brother Robin was still at war in the Far East for a few more months. I copied this photo to invite everyone in the cul-de-sac to come outside to sing Vera Lyn's *We'll Meet Again* to my (very poor) accompaniment on violin. It was good fun as someone came out with his ukulele, and another with their electric keyboard. By the time we'd got ourselves organised, we'd sung the song about six times!

During the summer when restrictions eased, the beaches and cliff paths around here became unpleasantly busy and all campsites were fully booked, but friends came and parked their camper van on my drive and we had barbecues in the garden. Later, when my brother Mike came to stay, we hugged through an unused plastic shower curtain!

This winter has been made more bearable as I had the use of a beach hut and have been swimming throughout the winter. It has become very popular here.

I keep in touch with **Alicia Holmes (Rolston)**, **Jane Tompsett (Hunter)**, **Amelia Trevethick** and **Charlotte Walpole**.

Keep safe and keep smiling everyone!

Lorraine Stanton (Martin) With turning 60 I have found a new lease of life. My husband and I have moved from our farm in Wiltshire and now live in Great Missenden, Buckinghamshire, close to our grandchildren. We have four and I LOVE being a grandma.

I'm also deeply in love with my garden, which currently is a rough, grassy mess, but I have great plans. I've never done anything like this before, having spent most of my life in the kitchen in one way or another, but my heart has found a new love in the soil, amongst the worms and the spiders. Alongside the veg patch, we have planted an orchard. This year's projects extend to having cut flowers and a rose garden in memory of the growing number of our family who are leaving this earthly life. Excited and blessed I am, and I wish you well in our 60s!

Stephanie Wolfe (Binder) This last year has been quite testing for all of us. Luckily, the son with pulmonary hypertension and husband with various long term ailments are no worse. Just don't measure my blood pressure!

Three of the children, a partner and their two cats came to spend lockdown with us, so the dining room became an office and I watched while they drank their way through our wine cellar and my gin supply!

As I work outdoors, I kept working throughout, but had difficulty in getting my fellow gardeners back to work as they didn't really understand that they could; so, for a month I rushed around as many gardens as possible, and persuaded our furloughed sons to mow, weed and prune too! Flo also kept working as she is a land agent, when not volunteering at the Nightingale Hospital as a member of the First Aid Nursing Yeomanry (known as the FANY'S). We only finally got rid of them all in November!

My 60th birthday celebrations were all cancelled but I did manage a pub lunch with some friends before the second lockdown. I have retired from being a school chaplain and also retired from the PCC after 33 years and from ministry after 20. I can now stalk the services of other local churches on YouTube or watch the Cathedral Service. No longer being responsible for raising the Parish Share is a huge weight off my shoulders. It has become increasingly challenging these days.

When the Westonbirt Jamboree actually happens, I will hope to see some of you there!

Section 47 (1977)

Section Representative:
Sally Kincaid (Franklin)

My first year taking over as Section Rep for Section 47, and a big thank you to everyone who has responded to my requests for news, especially those we haven't heard from for a number of years. **Kate Porter** gets the prize for the speediest reply – it came within 24 hours – most impressive. From Scotland to Australia...what a team! What a year.

Omolara Akiwumi I'm retired after working at the Italian Embassy in Accra for several years. I run my family estates together with my siblings. I've also partnered with my older daughter Briana and we have a clothing line together. She's a mother, actor, (she insists on being called an actor and not an actress!) writer and model. She also works for an online music distribution company called Ditto Music. She has a twelve-year-old son André. We all live together in Accra Ghana.

My youngest daughter Nikita is an artist and photographer. She loves painting, taking photographs and is avidly into IT as well. Currently she lives in North Carolina USA. She also occasionally works with an estate sales company and is in charge of sales for our clothing line Labukifitz.

Sara Alderman (Jefcoate) I am enjoying semi-retirement in Pembrokeshire. We have moved from the farm as Steve has also retired from farming and we now live 200 yards up the road in the village. Steve was jobless for a whole month and was then persuaded to become a county councillor. I have been doing a bit of bookkeeping to keep the old brain cells working and am now getting prepared to become a tuk tuk tour guide in south-west Pembrokeshire which looks like fun!

Sadly, we have not seen our daughter and family for a few months now and I really miss my girls, Megan and little Enid who is three years old. However, we had some brilliant news last summer as they have decided to move from the Wirral to Pembrokeshire this autumn. All very exciting.

It would be lovely to meet up again whenever we are allowed, and I look forward to seeing everyone again.

Sarah Blezard (Bouet) We are good and strangely enjoying lockdown as, being gardeners, we still have the freedom of the outdoors in the beautiful county of Cornwall - we live on the coast too which makes it extra special!

Fiona Dix (Bolus) Our experiences of this last year are probably much the same as everyone's; all locked down with nowhere to go. We've been very lucky to be untouched by the Covid virus here in the middle of nowhere. I am very blessed to have a wonderful garden to spend time in, two life-enhancing dogs and a new purpose in life: a gardening business!

So, I have made big changes this year. I had been really involved with parish matters via the Parish Council for some 15 years and after being summarily dismissed as surplus to requirements in February by my MP boss, following her promotion to Junior Minister, without even so much as a goodbye let alone a thank you, the realisation hit me that no one in authority really cares about individuals, nor local communities such as our 750-strong village, nor what parish councils say or do, nor how taxpayers money is used by the county, district nor South Downs National Park, so I was better off doing something for myself and choosing the projects *I* want to get involved with.... So, I signed up for a year's RHS course and set myself up to provide consultancy, ie helping people with planting ideas, full or partial designs or troubleshooting advice with tricky plants. I am loving it - even though the mud has gone on a bit this year!

Just occasionally I emerge to help with the latest "save the village" project. This year it is a huge project to try to buy the village pub as a community hub - an attempt to breathe life back into this otherwise dying rural village.

I have time to spend with Charlotte, who is working for her A Levels from home, whilst thinking hard about what she's going to be able to do on her gap year. Of course, they totally missed the entire lax season which I was sad about. I fancied one more year on the touchline at the old Merton tournament, now a much fancier affair, usually at Guildford Sports Park, with entrance charging, can you imagine! She's hoping to take up the offer of a place at Durham Uni to read Psychology and hopefully play loads there - that is, provided I can dissuade her from taking her horse with her!

My son Monty is happily out of sight and out of mind in Cardiff, in his second year, studying Economics; my sister **Elly (Weaver)** is locked down tightly in rural France, but Zooming with WB friends regularly, and with my father, housekeeping for his 91-year-old ladyfriend in London.

Katherine Hill (Cemlyn-Jones) As for everyone, this last year has been challenging. Working from home has had some hidden benefits, not the least a break from the delights of Premier Inns as our Care for the Family road tours have been on hold. I am still UK Director of the charity *www.careforthefamily.org.uk* and the pressure of successive lockdowns, as well as the trauma of bereavement, has meant our services have been more in demand than ever before.

In providential timing we moved to new headquarters in January 2019 and built a recording studio and auditorium. It's been a steep learning curve, but we have been brilliantly placed to produce new online events and material to help families. I have a new book out - *A Mind of Their Own - building our children's emotional wellbeing in a post pandemic world*. I started writing it before many of us had heard of Wuhan or the terms social distancing and shielding, but again the timing is perfect, as so many parents are feeling anxious about their children's wellbeing. There are lots of practical ideas for families and great cartoons. It's available from Waterstones and all good book shops (www.careforthefamily.org.uk/a-mind-of-their-own-book).

Family-wise we are doing OK - two of our boys and our daughter-in-law are doctors and so have been on the front line - in particular Henry, our youngest, who has been working on a Covid ward. Our grandchildren Ezra and Evangeline (Eva), both nearly two, bring such delight, and we can't wait for restrictions to lift. The old saying is true: "If we'd known grandchildren were so much fun, we would have had them first".

Patsy Howie (Wade) My husband Alan and I, with our dogs and cats, moved to Nolay, a small town in Burgundy, in 2017. We took early retirement, which took a while for me to get used to after so many years working ridiculous hours for one of the major management and IT consultancies. Now, after three years here, I can say that it's the best thing we've ever done. We are surrounded by beautiful countryside, most of which is vineyards. We have made so many friends, both French and English, and a neighbouring family of winemakers have pretty much adopted us, so we spend Christmas together and share in many family events.

The social life is excellent, although of course over the last year the typical meetings at bars, cafés and restaurants have been curtailed. We're just hoping that our local venues survive having been shut for so long. Some things have taken a while to get used to (French bureaucracy not least), but the people, the climate, the food and of course the wine are definitely enough compensation!

Cherry James (Lucas) Life has been very strange this last year. University teaching had to go online literally overnight; I have not been into the university since 17th March last year, working from home since. We teach online on MS Teams; very useful and efficient, but it has been exceptionally hard work for everyone, adjusting teaching materials, approaches, redesigning exams etc. and trying to engage students who one may never have met, and who don't want to switch their cameras on (possibly because they are in their pyjamas, sometimes because their broadband is not up to it).

We have stayed well, thank goodness, but one of my colleagues died of Covid early in the first wave, as have some other friends as the year has gone on. The hardest thing has been that Freddie is in Switzerland, so has been the other side of closed borders for much of the last year, and that Anna was first furloughed, then made redundant last year: her chartered surveying firm specialised in the hospitality industry so almost immediately had no work.

Having moved back in with us (from her flat a mile down the road) at the start of the first lockdown she was with us for over four months, which was lovely, and unexpected; but finding a new job in London proved very tricky, so, to cut a long story short, she is now working in Paris again having secured a job with a large UK property firm there. She went thinking that she would be able to come back here each month or so to keep up with her London friends and see us, but of course that idea is well and truly on ice for the foreseeable future, which is hard. At least she managed to move over there before the end of 2020 and the completion of Brexit; it would have been infinitely more difficult for her if she had not managed to do it beforehand. So, at the moment we are living a very quiet life and just hoping that borders reopen as soon as possible.

Serena Jones (Walthall) I have settled into being a hermit quite easily over the last year, and am managing to do many things online, from Pilates to playing bridge and the inevitable Zoom calls and quizzes. I've been able to continue singing with a few friends from choir. We choose a song, find a backing track on YouTube to sing to, and then record ourselves individually, with the backing track. We then have to send it to someone who puts them all together and sends us the collated version. We call ourselves the Lockdown Sopranos and have a somewhat dubious CD of all the 20 songs we did last year! No, you can't have a copy!

I am particularly lucky to be living with my husband and two daughters, both in their twenties. Neither of them would choose to be living at home at their age, unable to have a social life, but at least they have mum and dad's listening ear on tap! Kim (26) has been working at Osborne Clarke for three years and is hoping to do a master's degree at Bristol University next year. She has put it off twice, due to circumstances, but is now desperate to have a change of scene. Vanessa (22) was forced into a change of direction by Covid, as she was unable to work as a sailing/windsurfing instructor in the Med last year. She landed herself a job at FareShare, the food distribution charity, where she and I had been volunteering since the first lockdown in March 2020. She is thoroughly enjoying it and is now my boss when I go in on Tuesday afternoons! I haven't been able to do my volunteering for Riding for the Disabled for the last year, so it is nice to have another charity to be involved in.

We didn't get a holiday abroad last year, but did manage to choose the absolute best weather for a week at the Cotswold Water Park in September. With blue sky and sunshine for the whole week, we didn't need the Mediterranean. We did an hour or so of water sports each day, which tended to be open kayaks/canoes or stand-up paddle-boarding and then did various walks and generally explored the area.

Our woods also give us a good project to get stuck into. Tree planting and managing is essential work, so we are free to go whenever we need. It gives us a fantastic excuse for fresh air and exercise, in a completely Covid-free environment. We can't take friends and family during lockdown, but at least Dave and I can get out. We do feel very lucky.

Corinna Kershaw (Chown) I am living in a cottage in North Pembrokeshire with two dogs and eight hens. I now have five grandchildren all of school age. Covid has meant the closure of my thriving micro B&B so I launched new business, Caer Candles (*www.caercandles.com*) online in November, helped by the other family entrepreneurs. The candles are eco and vegan friendly, and have a range of beautiful fragrances. The plan is to run both the B&B and Caer Candles in tandem post-Covid.

I'm also back in the regulatory world after a break, sitting as a lay panelist for another healthcare regulator. My main activities are gardening, including growing many of my own vegetables, singing with the local Welsh choir of which I'm the chair, and I'm still working towards being a fluent Welsh speaker. I'm also a trained reading dog handler, taking Hugo (one of the dogs) into two primary schools to help children with their reading, and into Pembrokeshire College during exam times to help calm the nerves of students.

My son Joe (36) has two boys, and works for an exam board, which keeps him very busy. Naomi (36) and her husband Rob have enjoyed homeschooling their three children and expanding their business (www.frogandgnome.com) through the pandemic. My youngest, Nick (33) just made it back to the UK from Guatemala before the first lockdown and has been here with me ever since, trail running on the coast paths and hills, and keeping his business alive, and fit for the post-Covid world, whilst doing a Master's in International Development at SOAS.

Sally Kincaid (Franklin) Like everyone, 2020 was the year that was for me. I returned to Australia, from two weeks with my parents in Shropshire, in mid-March 2020. Fortunately, I got back just in time to avoid the mandatory and punishing regime of hotel quarantine. Small mercies!

From that point onwards, my team and I all worked from home – 9.30am Zoom teleconferences for the whole team every morning and, being in the health sector, the workload exploded exponentially. It was quite amusing at first – the wheels of justice were turning in the dining room (commandeered for Andrew's office, where he conducted his hearings via Zoom) and me in the study next door trying to negotiate the twists and turns of a health system under pressure (and keep the noise down during the aforesaid hearings). Fortunately, the Courts allowed Andrew to return to Chambers for hearings after about a month so we both retained a modicum of sanity!

Jack (27) was with us during the first lockdown. Having completed his post-grad law degree at the end of 2019, he had just started working as a Judges' Associate in the County Court (who were also all working from home on Zoom) when the first lockdown hit. He made sure to be in Melbourne in his shared house for the second lockdown – a bit more fun for him than being with us full time, I suspect. These lockdowns have been so very hard on the young. He has just this week started a new job with a law firm called Slater and Gordon, working in their class actions division.

Lots of travel cancelled last year, and for we in Australia that continues into this year. We still aren't allowed to travel overseas - maybe by the end of 2021... maybe. I was supposed to be going to Tokyo and Dublin with work this year, which won't be happening, and multiple interstate trips have been put on hold. Seriously though – that's such a small price to pay and pales into insignificance when one considers the pain and suffering that has been going on in the world. We are hoping to have our Covid vaccinations by September... seems a lifetime away.

Again, thanks to all who have contributed below, and as our Kiwi neighbours say "Kia Kaha" (Stay safe).

Fiona Leith (Goodbody) Like most people, I haven't been anywhere this year but the garden is looking amazing! We worked on it for the whole of 2020 and completed projects which we have talked about for years. Frances came home last March and stayed until mid-August and then again from December to February, so seven out of the last 12 months at home. It has been lovely for us, but not great for her. Thankfully, she has been working the whole time - not easy for a professional horn player with no live music allowed, but musicians have been very inventive and entrepreneurial.

The other two have also been working throughout, Donald on Covid wards in London, and Will on old cars. We have relentlessly walked all over our local area and are longing to stretch our legs elsewhere. Both my book groups have survived on Zoom, and online bridge has been a wonderful way to spend time with friends. The jigsaws are worn out and I have taken up tapestry. We had one outing, on a lovely sunny July day, to the Hauser and Wirth garden and gallery in Somerset. It was such a treat and the café there is brilliant.

Frances and I think we had mild Covid last April and Donald definitely had it, symptom-free, in May. The others have either dodged it somehow or not had symptoms. I have been invited for my first vaccination next week. The other highlight of the month is finally getting a dentist appointment to fix a tooth which snapped in half in May and has been held together with chewing gum and string ever since. Strange times!

Gloriana Marks de Chabris You may/may not know but I run various property businesses – single family rentals, developments (converting offices to flats and houses) and now commercial property to hold as an investment asset class. I have a small team that work on the rental side (currently all work remotely) so I can come up with ideas for the conversions or buying commercial property. I had zero experience when I started as I had spent years in financial services/consultancy. I now often find I know more about capital limits, credit committees, etc than the person on the other side.

Every now and then I think that I am not doing anything and then I remember that I have a dilapidations review under way at a commercial property, planning in for converting two listed buildings into two houses, various refurbs and purchases of single family homes starting or under way, etc. and then I sit back and say to myself, "Enough".

I have also started writing my "Musings over Proper Tea" (property) and getting the posts out on LinkedIn. They are just quick thoughts on various aspects of property development and management. I don't have an agenda; I am not trying to sell a course; I am just talking about things (like Death in the Time of Covid) because no one else is… and maybe someone out there would like to work on a project but doesn't know how. You never know until you try…

Pandemic continues to be challenging. Graeme and Rosella bailed out of London and came to Hampshire at the start of the first wave. We were all sharing the same truly awful broadband. They have now gone back and at last BT have promised to bring fibre sometime in the next few months – seems it involves wires on poles (needs planning permission) and then digging trenches through the next-door field and garden. I am not holding my breath!

Graeme continues on the board of the International Fund for Animal Welfare (IFAW) which used to involve meetings on the east and west coasts of the US. No sooner did they plan a trip to Kenya than Covid scuppered their plans! He keeps himself out of too much mischief…

Rosella is in her final year at the New College of the Humanities which is now part of Northeastern University in the US. NCH is a tiny college in London modelled on an Oxbridge one and so everyone knows everyone. Most were overseas students so when Covid came along, they all fled home. I think she will be glad when this learning phase is over and she can start to change the world. Little interest in property it seems – but I am not pushing it.

The only good thing out of Covid has been that I now "see" (via Zoom) more of my sister and brothers and their families and their pets, than I have in years.

So, it's been "head down and focus" for a bit and, unfortunately, I expect it will be like this for the immediate future – but at least spring is on its way!

Wendy McWilliams Still living in Bedford and the children have been home through this Covid horror. Not sure when they will be fully off the payroll, so retirement is still a distant dream. My naughty spaniels are still noisy and badly behaved. (I blame the owner!) Only time they didn't bark was when some low-life climbed into my garden to steal my brand new bike. Other than that, I hope everyone is well and looking forward to vaccinations and vacations.

Tina Panton (Galanis) We went into lockdown on Symi in March 2020, and apart from a few weeks in the summer we seem to have been in it ever since… blah blah blah. Our island has remained Covid-free thus far, and the vaccination programme seems to be going well now that supplies are available. We're both getting our first jab this week (not too often age is an advantage) and our second in three weeks' time - yippee! Very excited! A lot of people here are loath to be vaccinated - OMG the crazy conspiracy theorists! - but most people realise their social and working lives will be severely limited if they choose not to have the vaccine. We're hoping to have a tourist season AND stay safe this summer. *www.symivillagalanis.com* - just a small plug!

We attended our first Zoom wedding at the end of May. Our eldest daughter Anna got married to her lovely wife Erica at Erica's parents' home in New York. Even though we couldn't be there, it still managed to be a joyful experience, 74 people watching and taking part from every corner of the earth! Strange, but you could feel the same kind of happiness from all those people "at the wedding" as you get at an "in person" wedding. It was a beautiful day, the garden looked beautiful, they both looked beautiful, I cried, we all drank champagne!

The rest of the year I seem to have spent watching *Olive and Mabel*, *Twinsthenewtrend*, *Jeeves and Wooster*, and listening to old BBC radio plays, all on YouTube. Hugh Laurie singing "Forty-seven ginger-headed sailors" raises a smile every time. Just asked David if he could think of anything else that happened last year, and he can't either! Hoping for better things for us all 2021, stay safe. Lots of love to you all. Tina.

Kate Porter (Bullock) Life continues here in Stirling, just in a very quiet way! We have all found 2020 to have been a very strange year, but personally we have been largely very fortunate. All of the family are healthy and safe, and mostly able to work from home. I myself am retired from teaching and am very fortunate that our children are all doing huge amounts to keep us safe and do shopping, and fetching and carrying for us, so that we can pretty much isolate.

We are so very thankful for a lovely garden to allow us to exercise and enjoy being outdoors safely. Have nothing of note to report, since we have rarely been anywhere other than with the family bubble.

Keep safe everyone, enjoy what you can and hope for a much brighter future for us all, as the vaccines begin to have an effect. Best wishes to all, virtual hugs for all who need one, and I am always here if anyone wants to chat.

Leigh Ralphs (Davidson) As a Type 1 diabetic for nearly 40 years (plus other issues!) I started to unofficially semi-shield in February 2020 before we were all locked down the first time. Fortunately, my husband was able to work from home and during the spring and summer we were blessed with lovely sunny weather, so I spent a lot of time in the garden. I was able to get online food deliveries, and Christmas shopping was done online as well, so I didn't feel as if I was missing out too much.

Thankfully our four-year-old working Cocker Monty needed walking twice a day, so that kept us reasonably active, and I continued with Pilates via YouTube (even persuading Guyon to join in!). My golf lessons were sporadic, but I am now looking forward to the spring and taking it up again, this time with the help of Guyon who retired at the end of December. With the end of the job came the end of the house we had lived in for the past ten years. We have bought a cottage in a small village "over the hill" and moved in at the end of the year, once a two-storey extension had been finished. Never again, she says! Buying a seventeenth-century cottage comes with many challenges – as I write we are putting in a new sewage treatment plant to replace the old septic tank. It does seem never-ending. However, we love the house and location as we are semi-rural but can walk into the village across the fields.

Charlie and James have both been teaching online when necessary. Sadly, we have seen very little of them because of Covid – we managed a ski trip to France *en famille* just before the virus arrived but otherwise it has been a difficult year being apart so much. Thank goodness for Zoom! It's also been difficult for my mother who has vascular dementia and is now in a home. Visits have felt like prison visits as she is behind a screen quite a long way off, I am wearing PPE, and she hasn't got a clue what is going on! She will be 100 next month.

Thankfully, we have now had our first vaccination and are looking forward to the second, hoping that we will be able to get to Spain once again – it's been two years, as all our trips were cancelled.

I do hope that we will all be able to get together at Westonbirt in May 2021 for a massive reunion!

Debbie Ronchetti Sorry to see the end of lockdown in a way. Being a bit of a recluse, it's suited me. I work from home as a court transcriber these days, so I'm reassured to learn that the courts are three years behind on hearings! Should keep me busy until retirement and beyond!

I live for my beautiful dogs. As long as they have food, treats and a warm bed (to share with me, when I'm allowed), my life is complete.

Penny Sloman (Sheard) My news is not very exciting as usual… I am still living in London and playing lots of tennis when I am allowed to and now play Padel tennis too which is great fun. There is a lot of online bridge but I try not to play too much.

My two sons are living in Sydney and one in New York and I finally got my husband back from Saudi on 1st April this year.

I am still mentoring men who come out of HM Prisons, which feels like useful work in trying to help them avoid reoffending, and I'm training to work for another charity called Shout.

Delivering food for the local Foodbank every Thursday is another thing I'm involved with; it's in demand more than ever before in this pandemic.

I also teach children to read over Zoom through another local charity, which is rewarding and fun. Oh, and I also did the Association newsletter with **Semmi** and **Leigh**... so talented! All the work I do is for Christian-based charities so there you go. Basically, I am a born-again Christian without going to church!

Nicola Vollkommer Sperry It's always great to catch up with what everyone is doing through the Association News each year - it makes a great read, and how lovely to be able to touch base once a year after so many years!

Our lives here in Germany, like everyone else's, came to a halt with the first Covid lockdown a year ago. We tried to make the best of a situation which was harrowing at times, being grateful for the good things in life, and trying to help those who were badly hit with the crisis.

I was able to use some of the time for writing - finishing my new novel, writing a handbook for young people about handling social media, and giving my book on raising children an update. School was on and off, depending on the Covid rules, which continue to change from week to week. I helped with caring for the children of key workers and appreciated the opportunity to get out of the house in the mornings. Church meetings were able to continue for the main part, with the handbrakes on, and with the help of Livestream. We are no fans of the digital world, but we had to become experts overnight! And rapidly concluded that there is definitely no replacement for live encounters!

Our grandchild count will have nearly doubled by the summer! Jessica and Debbie both had baby girls last December, and Stefan and his wife Johanna, as well and Dani and Linda, are expecting babies in the summer, which brings us up to nine altogether. We feel very blessed and enjoy the little ones so much. Happy to have most of them nearby and even in the same church, and to be in close Facetime contact with Dani and Linda in Berlin. Always great to hear about Westonbirt, also to be in contact with some via Facebook.

Jenny Webb (Binder) Strange year for everyone; for us it meant a full house from March through to October - a long time since we experienced that, and six adults (we had James' fiancée with us as well) is different to two adults and three children. On the plus side, they did lots of cooking, contributed to cost of gin and food and were good company. On the downside, every room was a workspace, so John and I were largely confined to the kitchen until the weather improved and we could go outside! An experience we will look back on positively with shared memories.

We all had Covid at the start, but thankfully not badly, and now here we are a year later, and I am helping with the vaccination programme, the only thing this country seems to have got right. We finally decided to replace our beagle, Tully, who died two and a half years ago - and like a bolt of lightning Tazzie has entered our lives and galvanised us! Like childbirth, you forget what a puppy is like after years of an older dog, but on balance it is a good thing! James and Lois had to cancel their wedding, like so many others, but did manage to buy a flat in the July-September period of freedom, so moved back to London in October. As for many, social life has been reduced to interaction in small squares via Zoom or Facetime - but the only thing I really missed was my choral singing, so hope we can get back to that in the summer.

Veronica Weller Jones Sorry, but I don't have any news for the **Westonbirt Association News**, given the exceptional Covid year we have had and all the lockdowns, which are still ongoing. We have been playing it safe and have been entrenched at home, and escape for local walks daily. Looking forward to living in a world with a bit more normality and the freedom to roam!

Mary Wickenden I have been living and working in sunny East Sussex now for two and a half years, which I can't quite believe. Working at the Institute of Development Studies, which is part of the University of Sussex (not that I have been to the campus more than once in the past year) but crazy busy trying to run adapted research projects and some online teaching from my bright red study in my house in Lewes. Work is a bit of a nightmare and I am seriously plotting my escape sometime in the next year or two.

Living in Lewes is lovely, but not enough time to do all the tempting nonwork things I want to. I have succumbed to a lockdown puppy - a fluffy bundle of cheekiness called Winnie (www - Winnie the Woofer Wickenden) who is stopping me working so hard and getting me out on those beautiful South Downs. Wuff!

Section 46 (1976)

Section Representative:
Jean Stone (Borritt)

Nicola Capewell (Wilson) Nicky said "My husband Ian had his jab almost three weeks ago and is back volunteering at St Cross Hospital so does regular lateral flow tests. Laura and Stan are in the process of cancelling all their March bookings for their Pembrokeshire camping and glamping business but hoping Easter will be OK, whilst Nick and Ali continue to work as normal. Roll on spring, I say! Sorry but have got absolutely no other news worth reporting this time."

Susan Hopkins (Heather) I had lost contact details for Susan but was able to reconnect after she used the Westonbirt Association Facebook page. Susie said, "The last time I wrote, we had just moved to Somerset to be near our daughter and were about to embark on our house renovations. I am pleased to say that we managed to complete them just prior to the first lockdown in March 2020.

"Well, what a year it has been! Roger and I chose to lockdown on 7th March, just prior to the Government announcement. Roger is classified as vulnerable, and we felt it was the right thing to do under the circumstances. So here we are exactly one year later as I write this, still in lockdown but still talking to each other! We have spent time sorting through all our cupboards and decluttering, making changes to the garden, planting, repairing fences, erecting new fences, and giving ourselves a project most days.

"Like most people we have embraced video calls with family and friends, monthly family quizzes and generally keeping in touch the best way we can. I have probably written more letters this year, which is a little strange when there is not much to write about, but it has been good to keep in touch. Hopefully, we will all look back on 2020/21 as a time of pulling together and being kind to each other. We will embrace the new normal and value holding hands and hugs with family and friends again soon."

Claire Savoca replied from her home in Geneva. "Last year, as for us all, was a unique year. A year of confinement. I took the opportunity to catch up with all my bits and pieces that had been on the back burner. Then there was (Biblical) Hebrew. I started learning the language two years ago. Fascinating. Every character has a number and a picture to it which makes it a mathematical and pictorial language as well. Then there is the hidden code in the Biblical text with the equal sequencing system. Really Fascinating. Then there was the writing of my poems. A year of confinement but I kept myself busy.

Jean Stone (Borritt) For me, it has certainly been a challenging year in every respect. The death of a friend in his late fifties early on in the first lockdown brought home all too sadly the seriousness with which Covid needs to be taken. The first lockdown was comparatively easy. It was a novelty being at home and having no excuse not to get on with long delayed jobs and a good clear out. It was also an opportunity to catch up with friends by phone or letter, read many books, start a tapestry, and do several jigsaws.

I was able to get out and do lots of walking, exploring local footpaths and lanes that I had never been down before and getting myself lost on occasion. By the end of the year, I had completed over 1,000 "Boots on" miles. I was fortunate to be able to squeeze in five days in Northumberland between the first and second lockdowns. Although the seaside villages were fairly busy, the vast open beaches were virtually deserted and I walked for hours in glorious sunshine, stopping to eat crab sandwiches, paddle in the shallows or even to enjoy a bracing swim. I stayed in a lovely, Covid-secure B&B in Alnwick and the short break recharged my mental batteries, making it easier to cope with the second lockdown. While away I managed to meet up for a day with my eldest daughter Eleanor, who had joined a GP partnership in Jarrow earlier in the year. The pair of us had a great afternoon paddle-boarding on the Coquet river. It was so hot that it was a genuine pleasure to fall in for a cooling dip.

In September I had a freak accident in my garden. I tripped and fell forehead first into the open wheelie bin. I sustained a deep cut to my head and whiplash from the force with which I hit the bin. Unfortunately, the care and treatment I received at the time was less than optimal, so I have been left with a lump above my brow and a bigger scar than was necessary. It took 11 weeks for all the surgical glue to be forced out of the wound.

I also rattled my brain and upset my blood pressure for several weeks. It was quite a shock to realise that I am not invincible. Now that I have recovered, I am working as a vaccinator in a mass vaccination centre. It is hard work but satisfying to know that I am contributing in some small way to getting the country back on its feet again and returning to whatever the new normality turns out to be.

Baby-sitting my granddaughter Martha one day a fortnight continues to give me great pleasure. At 20 months she is developing a real personality and keeps us all amused with her antics. She will be joined by a sibling in late August, so we will have to see how that pans out! Eleanor has just postponed her wedding for a second time, having just missed out on the increase in numbers from 15 to 30. The new date is in early December so I am sincerely hoping that it will be a case of third time lucky. This third lockdown has felt much harder. Although I am still walking and am lucky to be able to do so, all the footpaths are becoming too familiar and routine and I am looking forward to trips further afield and to being reunited with family and friends, as indeed are we all.

Section 45 (1975)

Section Representative:
Susie Younger (Goodbody)

Anne Millman I anticipate there'll be very common themes in the newsletter this year, but am sure the network of (increasingly) old school friends will have formed part of our mutual resilience. My focus has continued to be on caring for my husband, Hans, as we continue our lives together after his year-long stay in intensive care and hospital in 2018/19.

Alongside, I've been lucky enough to maintain a working life for various cultural organisations, learning fast about "blended learning" and engaging in constant planning – unplanning – replanning. Meanwhile, this little corner of Oxfordshire continues to be a source of much comfort and pleasure.

Fiona Stokes (Tobin) Currently staying with my mum in Oxfordshire and caring for her and taking care of the house, with help from my brother and lots of support from husband Chris. Mum had been surviving lockdown, with regular visits from James and me, but suddenly her spine fractured due to osteoporosis. She was recovering from the pain and immobility when she was suddenly admitted to hospital with sepsis. Thankfully antibiotics have worked to eradicate infection, but I am still at her house, awaiting a hospital care package to commence.

Lockdown in March 2020 found us at Bagshot with Matt and Ben living at home. Fast forward to March 2021 and they are both living with girlfriends, Ben working from home in Wokingham, and Matt studying for his master's in London. Ollie and girlfriend are about to exchange contracts on a modest property in Cheshire and he is working from home whilst Claire teaches, online and in the classroom.

Lockdown seemed to cause a bout of depression for me, but I got medication from a sympathetic GP (phone consultation) and it helped me to face anxieties over Mum. I found my way back to keeping busy and just as well, given Mum's current situation. I am tired and don't sleep well, and fed up with lockdown, but I am one of millions!

Miss friends, miss social gatherings, miss theatre, opera, concerts, singing (last attempt was with church choir outside in the dark and rain, trying to record carols whilst socially distanced, with the rector livestreaming the carols to the village via Facebook). Tennis is on the horizon for 29th March but who knows if it will actually be allowed?

Managed to get to our holiday lodge in Anglesey last August but no sailing club, and no socialising and only occasional precious meetings on beaches with cousins. However still managed some lovely walks and even some swimming in the sea.

Enjoyed some dog walks last year with **Trudy Evans (Wardle)** in the Reigate area, and **Ali Cheeseman (Dorey)** near Pangbourne and last saw **Lizzie Bennett (Phelps)** in London in early October when I visited for breakfast and lunch whilst waiting to pick up Chris after a minor procedure at St Mary's, Paddington.

Have spoken to **Virginia Mullan (Sanders)**, **Lorna Hooley (Lovell)** and emailed **Jane Golding (Gaffney)** and **Anne Millman**, but obviously have not been able to see them. Saddest of all is the loss of **Jane Seymour** who died on 8 December, having been diagnosed less than two years previously with motor neurone disease.

Clare Williams and I were invited to her funeral in Norwich in early January on a freezing cold and foggy day, where Clare delivered a very moving tribute. Jane's partner Gordon had organised a horse-drawn cortege to the crematorium from the church. The photos I took of royal blue plumes, four grey horses (as in white), and a white-framed glass carriage with her coffin, which reflect the memory of the black cortege of Jane's own mother, whose funeral Jane had invited me to attend some years ago.

Jane Sinclair from the year above us has also died. There was an obituary in the *Church Times*.

On the more cheerful side, Chris has discovered that he enjoys growing things in pots in the garden and our leaky roof has been mended, guttering replaced and all new and shiny!

Susie Younger (Goodbody) We have had one of our sons and his wife staying for nearly a year now with their baby son, now a year old, which has been fabulous and kept us on our toes and never bored! The house they have been renovating should be ready in about June.

Our oldest son was supposed to be getting married on 1st May (cancelled) and they are going to try to arrange a new date soon for a service and have a party next year.

Farming has continued as normal too, so we consider ourselves very lucky but still longing for it all to be over, lockdown-wise.

Section 44 (1974)

Section Representative:
Elizabeth Battye (Jones)

Elizabeth Battye (Jones) I have become a grandmother for the second time as my daughter Claire had a baby girl, Freya, in November, sister to Edward. Unfortunately, we have not been able to see much of them in person due to the lockdowns, so I am looking forward to the restrictions being eased. My son, Thomas, lives nearby with his wife, which has been wonderful as at least we have been able to see them on the doorstep.

Tina Cook (Jenne) I was sad to see the announcement of the deaths of **Felicia Leman** and **Jane Sinclair** this year. A chance to remember them both from so many years ago and reminder of our mortality - not that we weren't reminded during 2020!

We've all learnt a lot this year. I'd never thought of teaching piano online, but with Zoom and FaceTime have found it works reasonably well. Instead of back-to-back lessons I find I need a five- or ten-minute break so that my brain can unscramble from the screen. It's been interesting to find out which age groups have most difficulty with the technology. It's not the adults, but younger children, who find it hard to concentrate when there isn't someone there in person. As we all are, I'm enormously looking forward to seeing students, friends, and family. I've certainly learnt to appreciate the smaller things in life.

The village churches round us have managed to continue using the phone for services, which is accessible to all ages, and if anything has enabled more people to take part.

Daughter Hannah has nearly finished two years as a junior doctor, some of the time in A&E, which has been challenging and fulfilling. She's taking a gap year in Australia, working in a hospital doing emergency surgery there with a group of friends (shark bites etc?!) before returning to UK and starting surgery training.

Mum remains in good spirits and is Zooming with the best of us at age 92! Her diary is fairly full with this, and Steve and I are in prime position to give technical support where needed.

Jennifer Denholm (Goodbody) While the weather was nice, I was able to have garden visits from the daughters with grandchildren which was really lovely. My sixth grandchild was born in July - very early but after some weeks in hospital is now doing extremely well.

I've become rather keen on gardening and have ordered a wheelchair accessible greenhouse… exciting! Now just waiting for a plinth to be laid before it arrives, and whizzing through seed catalogues!

My Mum just had her 91st birthday, but of course I wasn't able to see her- grrrrr! Luckily, Susie lives nearby and was able to take her a cake.

Julia Goss (Wilcox) This last year, as no doubt others have said, has been strange. I seem to have become the family dog kennels, with first my niece's dog for several months (whilst she was stuck in South Africa) and now my sister's dog whilst she gets back on her feet. Fortunately, we live close to the North Downs and what else can one do in a pandemic but go for walks?!

Luckily, touch wood, Richard and I have been well. One highlight of the year has been reconnecting with my WB study mates- **Lulu James, Tish Bush**, and **Elspeth Bolus**. We have had a regular WhatsApp video call every two weeks or so for almost the whole year. Inevitably laughing over shared school memories and supporting each other through the trials and tribulations of lockdown. The years have just melted away.

Pauline Jackson (Garrett) Not a good year for me. Having lost a good friend, **Felicia Milicevic (Leman)**, to cancer, I too have cancer (myeloma) plus another incurable disease called amyloidosis. Have been undergoing chemo for the myeloma. Amyloidosis affects all the major organs of the body and so I am being treated for heart, lung, liver, kidney, and gastric complications. I live by my brother, and my youngest son lives with me, so they have been able to help out as I am extremely vulnerable to Covid.

Paul and Laura live in London and we talk regularly. They are marathon training this winter and have already raised over £2,000 for the amyloidosis charity. Eldest son Stephen lives in Spain with his family. I miss going to my home in Spain and hope that I can return there one day. Only time will tell. Everything is crossed!

Play Scrabble online with **Charlotte England (Wren)** on a daily basis. Keep in touch with **Tish John (Bush), Carolyne Buck (Armstrong), Tina Cook (Jenne), Katharine Saunders (Ryle-Davis), Carol Pusey (Cleal), Jane Fisher (Thornton)** and **Elspeth Weaver (Bolus).** Need to organise a reunion, I think!

Patricia John (Bush) Well what a year! Firstly, I'd like to send best wishes to everyone, especially anyone whose health has been affected by this dreadful pandemic. We never learnt about this sort of thing when we at school, did we?!

The John family have been lucky enough to stay well so far and we even managed to get away for a last-minute booking week when the first lockdown ended – in Cornwall! Always a favourite for everyone as long as the littles sleep! Soooo good to be out!

During the pandemic, we, being in Wales, were treated differently to England which caused several cancellations and a certain amount of Granny-envy, the other Grannies being in England. We did manage to celebrate our fortieth wedding anniversary in September with the family which was great.

Then Christmas was meant to be in Newport, (we take it in turns) and of course that was cancelled just before – I have to say all very difficult to cope with. Nick and I had far too much turkey and unwrapped Christmas presents for 10! We decided to go for a swim in the sea on Christmas Day and I have to say it was fantastic – it set us up for a good but different Christmas Day! I can definitely recommend cold-water dipping (swimming is a bit of an exaggeration!)

The two eldest grandchildren, Llewy and Evie, started school in September. It started well. Then schools shut, so this term has been very hard for anyone coping with school-age children, and ours have been no exception. Especially with a younger sibling to deal with, generally getting in the way and spoiling anything that is half organised! I have been called in to help with the children as a last resort, which I have to admit that I accepted with enthusiasm. Haven't seen them all enough, but with all the difficult times the whole country has been through, we feel very lucky – so far!

Once again, I would love to see anyone, when allowed, who ventures into Wales. I will definitely try and make the May 2022 90th(92nd!) anniversary celebrations.

Margaret Miller Brown I wish I had some interesting news to share, but mostly I've just been hunkering down at home, trying to get through this. For the first several months, our two sons and their girlfriends were living with us, which was a lot of fun, but once they moved on, the isolation of the pandemic really hit us.

When the wildfires burned for months on the west coast of the US, we felt doubly isolated and claustrophobic, with smoke stretching a thousand miles in every direction from us. Some days, the sun never seemed to rise, the lights of the city stayed on during the day, and the sky glowed a dull orange. The fires subsided just in time for the most stressful presidential election of my lifetime, and I'm only now allowing myself to come down off my sense of constant alert. I'm in the garden now almost every day, appreciating each flower and hummingbird, and more aware than ever of how fragile everything is.

Best wishes to you and all our classmates for a healthy year ahead.

Elspeth Weaver (Bolus) Not much news this year. No real changes in my son's circumstances. Fred has bought a flat in Copenhagen - there is talk of a job in Paris. No work in Toulouse, so George and his partner will stay up in Paris for another couple of years. A lot of hard work on the farm for Oliver, but during the Covid pandemic he has done a roaring trade in selling his beef directly to consumers.

My big news is that I have obtained French nationality at last (dual nationality) which gives me a position of security vis à vis Brexit. I worked in the Tourist Office again last summer and they have asked me back this summer. Few foreign tourists, but masses of French from all over the country. I haven't managed to get to the UK for nearly 18 months now and miss travelling, like so many people. Have had regular contact on WhatsApp with my old study mates, **Tish John (Bush), Lulu James** and **Julia Goss (Wilcox)** during the pandemic, which has been a great pleasure and good for the morale.

Section 43 (1973)

Section Representative:
Sarah Thomas (Leslie)

Thank you to all for sending in news. It's lovely to hear from you.

Lorraine Clemie (Gibbs) It's been a strange year. I started a new job at a school for the deaf in Leeds. It's a new challenge and great to be back at work after a ten-month gap. Many speech and language therapists have been on respiratory wards with Covid patients. I don't know how people cope working in those environments. They must be very special people.

John, my husband, is well and came out of isolation the day before his 70th birthday, having got over Covid. I got it too and got out a few days later. We both feel very lucky to have had it without any lasting effects.

Miranda Godbaz (Stracey) Our son John was married over in California last month, which was just wonderful, although we couldn't be there in person. Isn't Zoom a great invention? My daughter Susannah and her husband Josh have welcomed into the world their new baby Amelia Daphne. They are doing really well. Our first grandchild, and we are loving every minute!

Zoe Littleton I managed to get back to France on 16th December and have been in Arles since then. I will be returning reluctantly to London at the end of February, to check for burst pipes, deal with any unpaid bills, and to get the vaccine. In any event, I need to leave France by the end of March because post-Brexit rules mean I am limited to 90 days in 180 days. I have the joys of three Covid tests (the English ones don't come cheap!) and ten days of quarantine to look forward to. I have no idea when I'll be able to get back into France again as Brits are not allowed at the moment. Bill will be staying in Arles for the time being, as he hates being in London, but he may be enticed back to get the vaccine as it looks like he won't be able to get it here. Life here in Arles isn't too bad – lots of bright sunny days. The town is missing its usual buzz as all cafés and restaurants are closed so there is not the usual street life. Shops are still able to open, and the twice-weekly food market is still going strong, so we are able to eat nice food, accompanied by nice wine – our cellar is overflowing! Tennis is allowed so I am playing three or four times a week, which is good fun, good exercise and also gives me the chance to have a chat with my tennis friends.

We bought a new car in August with the expectation that we would be able to do a lot of exploring France (and trips to Italy and Spain which aren't too far away) but of course the car is having to spend nearly all its time in the car park, being used as a sunbed by the local cats. I'm enjoying having time to read books, knit on our roof terrace in the sunshine, and generally be a lazy slob, but it will be great when (hopefully!) life returns to some sort of normality.

I've had a couple of Zooms with **Rekha Ghose** over recent months. She is fine and very pleased that Trump is no longer president! They came to stay with us in Arles a year or so ago which was great. Her two kids are both living in London. I catch up with **Tish Golding** from time to time on the phone but haven't spoken to her for a while.

Sarah Thomas (Leslie) It's been a very quiet year! I was working from home during the first lockdown, but am now back at the office, with social distancing measures in place. No bellringing in church towers has been possible for the last year sadly. However, we have been able to ring online with the help of a new program, *Ringingroom.com*. This has been wonderful, and I even wonder if it could be kept going after we are back in churches. Although completely different and quite sedentary compared to real bells, it might mean we could ring for longer in advancing years!

My sister **Jean Leslie** (Section 41) has not been able to visit us from Australia since the Covid outbreak. She is planning to come as soon as travel restrictions are eased. I have been in touch this year with **Tish Millen (Golding)** and with **Maryon Jeane (Howard).**

Section 42 (1972)

Section Representative:
Miranda Purves (Saxby-Soffe)

With my request for news, I included photographs of Gloucester House in 1969, plucked from the Facebook page, which were a blast from the past! Also, memories of jumping the snake-pit.

We were unable to proceed with our planned reunion in the autumn of 2020 but hope to be able to have a get-together as soon as we are allowed, and our hostess is willing! Many thanks for all the replies I received for news requests.

Jane Barrett Jane's husband has just had to have a hip replacement having gone from walking around quite normally at Christmas to barely being to hobble by the end of January. He was so lucky to be able to have it done privately as the NHS orthopaedic waiting list is the stuff of nightmares. As it is, they hope he will be fit for the holiday season, which like everybody else they are wildly looking forward to. Having been a teacher, Jane had some pointed remarks to make on the quality (and cost) of the teaching we received at Westonbirt!

Libby Coats (Clover) enjoyed the Gloucester photos and says they are all well and grateful to have a dog to take on daily walks to keep them relatively sane. Sometimes she sees my cousin fly past her (cousin has moved nearby and is in training for a marathon running week in the desert - mad!).

Sally Gesua (Clifford) is getting bored of daily walks, on-line bridge playing and teaching on-line singing (at first she worried about frightening the neighbours!) and eating/drinking/eating/drinking during these lockdown months. Her good intentions of sorting through all her junk have not really happened over the past year, and she misses her children and grandchildren.

Rosalie Goldingham has been much relieved to be able to revert to her maiden name after her fraught divorce. She was locked down with her daughter and family in London for much of March through May, and her second grandson Oscar was born in April. She treasures every moment with her small grandsons. She also moved house (only six doors away!) in the autumn so now has more space to have friends and family to stay – including WB pals once allowed! Her employment at Cafcass continues, as executive assistant for the two operational service directors. The pandemic had an extremely complex impact for Cafcass and the work of the family courts, so consequently she has been working full-time but is hoping to return to four days a week sometime. She would also love more time for tennis, swimming, singing, playing bridge etc. Not quite the same doing all this on-line!

Elizabeth (Lizzie) Jamieson (Holloway) let me know the sad news that **Kofo Majekodunmi** (full married name Kofoworola Aduke Vigo) died in October 2020. There is a lovely web page on ForeverMissed in her memory, which includes a house photograph from her time at Westonbirt. Lizzie has also spoken to **Carjack (Carol Jackson)** who is very well, and she has also been in touch with **Clare Jordan (Gore-Langton)**. Lizzie's own family news, apart from the challenge of Covid, is that her younger son Andy had a wonderful but tiny (Covid-style) wedding service in the Fisherman's Chapel on Jersey with a congregation of eight. Lizzie is now expecting their first grandchild in May.

Debbie Marr (Cheston) had to retrieve my request for news from her junk file, but was able to reply to say that there are advantages to getting old in that we have been offered our jabs and we could all be released to go off on holiday soon. Cypress nightclubs, anyone? She too is looking forward to any reunion we can have.

Miranda Purves (Saxby-Soffe) All my 2020 holidays were cancelled, including going to see the Passion Play at Oberammergau, which ironically was first put on by the inhabitants as thanks for deliverance from the plague. Coronavirus put a stop to it this time. Activities and events can now be planned for restart, so I am having to stir myself from torpor again. Being on a farm at least I was able to see people coming in to care for the animals during lockdowns, and internet shopping was a bonus!

Giulia Rhodes (Bartrum) retired from the British Museum at the end of November 2019 and spent the first lockdown volunteering for a charity doing food and pharmacy runs for people self-isolating, which kept her occupied and was a good way of getting out of the house. Since then, she has been busy with freelance work as an independent art historian - writing articles on Albrecht Dürer (in connection with an exhibition opening at the National Gallery in November, plus recording an interview for Melvyn Bragg's "In our Time" programme) and Edvard Munch, on whom she curated an exhibition at the British Museum in 2019. She keeps in regular contact with her old British Museum colleagues through the dreaded Zoom

- on which everyone is expert now! She has become over-familiar with all the parks in the Richmond/Twickenham area (her dogs have not) and says it would be lovely to meet up and see real people again. Hopefully we can manage that later in the year.

Joceline San had just had her first Covid jab but found lockdowns were getting tough. Like many, she did a lot of baking and feeding her neighbours with cakes.

Deirdre Waud (Ward) 2020 was a year of two halves for her and not just with the first and second lockdowns. At the end of April, Juliet gave birth to their first grandchild, Lyra Scarlett Isabella. Deirdre is nicknaming her Lucky Lyra because she arrived at 7.07pm on 27th April weighing 7lb (plus a bit). No signs of broodiness from Lucy yet but they have a handful of a new puppy, a German Pointer called Ludo (another L). They also had two great holidays which is more than most – skiing in Austria in February and three-and-a-half weeks on their new boat from the Scilly Isles to Lymington in August. The skipper had a broad grin on his face the whole time as they overtook boat after boat and the skipper's mate did too because the wind was rarely in front of the beam (whatever that means!).

After that they came down to earth with a jolt because Chris was diagnosed with myeloma at the beginning of September. It is a treatable, but not curable, bone marrow cancer which means he will be having some sort of treatment until at least June, but he is currently in good spirits and expects to be around for quite a few years yet. Deirdre also had a shoulder op at the end of September which meant wearing a sling 24/7 for 6 weeks with no driving (black cloud for her but smiles from all other road users!) but it is now improving, with lots of painful physio. Back to tennis in April.

Deirdre's father died just after Christmas aged 96, after a long and healthy life supporting the cigarette and drinks industries, as well as shunning vegetables and most forms of exercise. He was still living in the historic house that some went to, in the UVI, when Deirdre's parents invited us all to drinks on the way to see a play at Stratford. They had been there since 1957, so Gilly, Jane and Deirdre have been spending two days a week there every week for the past two months clearing out a lifetime's possessions. The end of an era.

Section 41 (1971)

Section Representative:
Jennifer Cope

Karen Broomhead (Fielding) My news: Inevitably, I'm afraid news is somewhat dull. We have survived lockdowns, but have missed family, friends, days out, eventing and our house in France hugely. We have become pretty adept at Zooms/Facetimes and Skypes, but it really is NOT the same.

The upsides – the garden has never looked so wonderful, and my daughter and her partner moved into one of our barns in July creating a very small family bubble. A summer party is now planned to cheer us all up.

I finally stepped down as a Governor of Westonbirt last March. I was honoured and very much enjoyed being able to represent the Association on the governing body for about eight years. How time flies. As you know, the school was sold and, in spite of Covid, seems to be going from strength to strength. It is a matter of some pride to me that this change was achieved, although it seems strange that there are now male Association members! We owe a particular debt to **Jen Greenwood**, fellow Governor, and former pupil, who played an enormous part in the negotiations. We were lucky to benefit from her expertise and impressive common sense!

I have tried to keep in touch with Westonbirt friends over lockdowns...**Di Farrington (Broughton), Jen Greenwood, Lally St Maur, Jennie Cope (Wells)**. Jennie and I recently hatched a plan for a 50th anniversary reunion of our year. It just cannot go unmarked! We had hoped to hold it at Westonbirt at the Association AGM, but this is now not possible. Therefore, we aim to hold a 'jolly good' party here at Bonhunt House on Saturday 9th October, all being well. It would be great to gather a big group and I can offer accommodation for anyone travelling a long distance. Details nearer the time, but, in the meantime, it would be good if you could let Jennie know if you are thinking of coming along. We need the network to work hard for us to make it a well-attended bash! Fingers crossed we continue to outwit Covid and that the hoped for easing of restrictions goes to plan.

Nicola Currie (Penley) Your email arrived on the day I finally told the College it is time to set my retirement date. I sense freedom and time to go on long exploratory walks with the dog... and of course my husband.

We have spent lockdown continuing with the major restoration project at our church. In the end I have raised over £340k! The project started as being about restoring the bells, silent for a hundred years, along with the organ and building a new ringing gallery. In June last summer we heard we had also won a grant to build a WC and kitchenette in the newly formed tower room made under the new ringing gallery. It has included over a thousand hours of volunteer time, and, thanks to Covid, much of that input has come from myself and Malcolm. Now I have to do all the paperwork to prove to the National Lottery that we met their targets which included an exhibition in a local museum and writing a local history book. I didn't write the book, thank goodness, but I do now know a lot more about museum exhibitions!

Ann Grundy (Briggs) Lockdown was kind to us, and my husband and I flourished with fewer demands on our time. It has enabled us to look at which things we consider important and has focused our energy in some different directions. We have kept well and loved being together, and have walked most of the surrounding countryside. Two of our daughters announced they were expecting, so this summer we look forward to two more grandchildren being added to the family, making ten in all.

Angie Newhaus (Low) My husband is currently the Australian Ambassador to the Netherlands. Our previous postings have included Nigeria and Zimbabwe, so it is quite a novelty for us to be in Europe in a non-English speaking environment. We are now expecting to be here until the middle of next year when Matthew will (hopefully!) retire. We have bought a house in the Southern Highlands of New South Wales, midway between Sydney and Canberra, so we will be able to keep in touch with friends and family in both places.

Covid has meant we haven't been able to get home to see our daughter in over a year and we suspect it will be another year before we do. The Netherlands has been hit very hard but to date we have managed to stay well.

Section 40 (1970)

Section Representative:
Jennifer Cope

Clare Keep (Morton) Two new grandchildren arrived last year. Hoping to go on riding holiday in Shropshire that was deferred from 2020. Hoping to get back riding at the end of the month. Like everyone else not much to report.

Clare also had very sad news of **Kofo Majekdumni** and a tribute to her can be found at *https://www.forevermissed.com/kofovigo/about*

Section 39 (1969)

Section Representative:
Louise Dixon

Ann Ayodele (Hodge) I think we are all pretty fed up of being locked-down by now. I had the Covid vaccine three weeks ago and it has injected me with some motivation, and I feel more energetic. The hardest thing is not being able to see our family, especially for those of us with grandchildren. I haven't hugged my daughter for a year now. A year in which she has given me a new granddaughter, who is nearly sitting up already.

Initially I was busy with new projects, brushing up my French, doing some creative writing and lots of naughty baking. But all those have waned with time. I am hoping to celebrate my seventieth in June with a trip to Scotland. We must live in hope for better times, and also to really valuing what is most important in life, spending time with friends and family. I am glad to say that during one of the more liberated periods during the year, I did manage to meet up with **Louise Dixon** and **Jan Carlisle** and it was a great pleasure to renew contact and to reminisce about our days at school.

Jan Carlisle Well, what a twelve months we've been through. I have really missed my many dance classes and the old body is feeling very stiff now.

I replaced my large brass musical instruments (euphonium and trombone) with a (smaller) flugelhorn. Hardly had a chance to get my lip in yet. Lucky neighbours!

I live on a farm lane and am able to walk in the countryside, and I have a lovely garden that takes up much time. There is a second grandchild to look forward to, due in June, and the knitted shawl is nearly done, courtesy of lockdown!

The first lockdown gave rise to making scrubs for the NHS, the second to making jam and lavender bags for Christmas, the third to making Seville marmalade and Seville gin. How very domesticated I have become. Oh dear! Oh well, all thanks to passing Domestic Science O Level.

Louise Dixon This has been a year of reviving many contacts and reliving some reawakened memories of Westonbirt, through taking over as Section 39 Representative. Many thanks to **Liz Jubb (Grant)** for her continuing help in my taking over the role from her. It has been very enjoyable to have faces brought to mind again, that had rather slipped into the distance during the 50 years or so since we all left Westonbirt. We have developed a Facebook page for our Section and have had a lot of fun collecting together photographs – both formal and informal – and have been pooling our memories on who was who and what the events in the photographs might have been. We're still short of a couple of house photos, but we live in hope that someone will unearth some long-forgotten gems!

From a personal point of view, it has been a year of great change. I have had a very long connection with South Africa, but we sold our house there about a year ago and returned to the UK, just as the first lockdown drawbridge was being pulled up. As others will comment, the first lockdown, during good weather, was not such a great problem and we enjoyed discovering the wonderful network of cycle tracks and tow paths in the vicinity of Derby, with the surrounding plethora of rivers and canals.

We were then able to pass onto Step Two, which was to establish ourselves in Italy. We chose to base ourselves in Puglia, the Heel of Italy, which has turned out to be a charming choice. In the delightful hill town of Locorotondo, in the Valle d'Itria, we are surrounded by ancient dry-stone walls, olive groves, vines, fruit trees, and artichokes. Along with other Brits all over the EU, we had a considerable scramble to go through all the necessary residence processes before the Brexit shutters came down. Perhaps the one we feared the most was failing to exchange our UK driving licence for Italian licences before 31st December 2020, and then facing the prospect of sitting the written and practical driving tests in Italian! We are delighted to have secured our right to live in Italy 365 days a year, but are obviously very sorry that our long-held plans to travel, from that base, into the rest of the Schengen Area, will be limited to 90 days in every half year. We hope to resume our attendance at music festivals and historic opera houses, across Europe, before too long.

Our ability to get to know Puglia and beyond has been severely constrained by the lockdowns in Italy, but we have enjoyed, again, getting to know the local area by bike. We are very much looking forward to travelling around Italy in due course. Italian is an elusive language. I can understand it pretty well, from having worked there in the 1990s, and having taken courses in, for instance, Taormina in Sicily, and also from my knowledge of Spanish and Portuguese, but it's just all too easy to speak Italian fluently-but-badly! Self-discipline is very much needed to get down to the details of the verbs and many of the words which are, in fact, quite different from their other Romance cousins.

As a person who has constantly travelled far and wide, I can hardly believe that I have not been on a plane for 12 months! When we shall feel safe returning to our favourite haunts in India and Africa I really don't know. The real test of the vaccines' effectiveness will come in the next few months. We are certainly suffering significant withdrawal symptoms and just hope that "normal service will be resumed as soon as possible"!

Liz Jubb (Grant) Covid has ensured that news this year will be very different from the normal reports!! I can't believe it's just on 12 months since we all went into lockdown. When I look at the diary for the first three months of last year, compared to what it is now, it is unbelievable: in fact, I don't know how we found time to breathe!

One thing which has proved of great benefit is the enforced slower pace, resulting in much more rest and fresh air. We actually hugely enjoyed the first lockdown, as there was no feeling of guilt at just relaxing in the beautiful weather, working in the garden, exploring previously unknown areas from our doorstep in the form of new walks and revelling in the peace and quiet of the countryside.

As time went on, so we decided we had better do some constructive projects, so Phil set up as painter and decorator and did nearly all the inside rooms, which was fantastic. He combined this with hard work on his allotment, so we had plenty of fresh produce through the summer and autumn with plenty in the freezer. I was not so productive, but did a lot more cooking and made great advances with my photography. Zoom, of course, has featured heavily and really come into its own in many ways, not least allowing us to enjoy magnificent talks in camera club by speakers from all over the world and whom we could never have hoped to hear in normal times.

Zoom has also been a lifesaver for keeping in touch with people, although I still find nothing wrong with just using the phone! The US elections provided plenty of entertainment, and having visited Washington on an extended visit in 2019, we particularly enjoyed seeing so much of that lovely city (although not so much some of the people living there!) The violent scenes in early January were quite shocking and it makes you wonder just what is going to happen in American politics.

We had planned to see family at Christmas but early in December Phil developed an abscess on a back tooth and our local dentist would not do anything except offer an appointment for the second half of January! The inevitable happened, resulting in an enforced visit to A&E, which was something we could have done without, and the dentist was obliged to do something…on 23 December! Nevertheless, Phil's son still came over on Christmas Day, which was lovely, and he and I had a huge English breakfast whilst Phil looked on with envy.

We have not yet got to the stage of doing endless jigsaws, but we have found the latest lockdown more trying than previous ones, mainly because we can't go anywhere. In normal times we regularly go to the coast, and I miss seeing the sea, but compared to what some families are going through, this is a trivial drawback.

We have been tremendously fortunate in that we live in a gorgeous area, have a good garden, and nearly always meet people we know on our walks, on whom we can practice using our vocal cords!

YouTube has provided us with some excellent culture (which we would, I am sure, otherwise have missed) and the library has given us superb service throughout all the lockdowns. So far, we haven't put on weight, despite all the extra home cooking, and having completely mastered the art of online shopping, we are not short of anything to eat, drink or wear.

So, for us, this last year has been something of an adventure where the complete change in lifestyle has reminded us of how much we had become slaves to the diary, which prevented us from doing what we moved down here to do, which was retire! Like everyone, we hope that later this year we will see a return to more normal living, which will be such a relief to so many families and businesspeople. Meanwhile, many thanks to **Louise Dixon** for acting as our rep: a small group of our year has been in regular email contact through the lockdowns which has been great fun and brought back many memories.

Joanna Leadbetter (Salz) What a year! We happened to be in North Cornwall when the first lockdown began and have remained there pretty much throughout. At least it felt as if that pure sea air might have seen the virus off and for the first time for years the beaches here have been so empty they have been a delight. The early days were spent maximizing our one piece of exercise by striding across the sand. Just never allowed to sit down…

It's been a time for bringing out the camera – egrets, rocks, waves, oyster catchers, sunsets all snapped. Then capturing the same subjects again, the next day, when the sea might have changed colour, or the birds might have slightly changed their poses.

And never have we watched so many films. Comedies, thrillers, dramas, obscure foreign films… and even time to watch old Poirot mysteries and to see if we could remember whodunnit!

But in the background, there has always been the reality of the killer virus - not ever knowing where it might be - and the myriad of tragic stories across the world or closer to home.

But we are so lucky have survived it and to have been able to slow the pace right down ... to enjoy the simpler pleasures again - a hot bath, a cup of tea, or the fact we're still here!

Jill Powell (Fawkes) wrote: There may not be much news for this past strange lockdown year, but this is to let you know that I am alive and well and enjoying life in Farnham.

I spent most of the time walking the dog during the three lockdown periods, plus gardening, online grocery shopping, cooking (making marmalade was a good diversion in January), washing my hands, and cancelling or postponing dates in my diary. Funnily enough, I never got round to my two planned projects: learning Spanish or knitting! But I bought a bread-making machine in November for the second lockdown, and I've really enjoyed baking bread and rolls. Clearing out clothes, papers, tidying cupboards… I'd rather be playing tennis.

During one of my tidying up sessions, I came across a box of old photos from Westonbirt days - lots of memories from 50+ years ago. It was fun identifying the faces and remembering those "good old days"! Plus, the bonus of getting in touch with several school friends again. I have posted the photos on our Westonbirt 1969 Facebook page, if you feel like a trip down memory lane.

But last summer when restrictions were relaxed, it was great to be able to play tennis again, visit National Trust Properties and Wisley, see friends and family outside and even go away for a few days.

Our summer hols were spent on the Isle of Wight, during the heatwave in August, and we swam in the sea every day.

We went up to Scotland in September and stayed in Northumberland on the way home, with a day's walking along Hadrian's Wall which was stunning. Meeting up with **Louise Dixon** for lunch on our way south was great fun, we had not seen each other since 1969! A visit to the rewilding project at Knepp Castle in October was fascinating, like an African safari experience, but in Sussex. In December, we had a few days in Cornwall, then the Isles of Scilly over Christmas - a good place to celebrate my "new 50th" birthday.

Section 38 (1968)

Section Representative:
Chris Shaw (Morris)

Alison Andrews (Morgan) We've been getting off lightly from Covid Year (now evidently stretching into Covid Era). It's a matter of luck to be too old for a responsible job, and we're privileged to live in the countryside with a reliable broadband connection and ample space for social distancing. I'm truly grateful, and lost in admiration for the people who've been putting so much effort into caring for victims of the virus and producing vaccines to keep us all safe.

Two good things that happened in 2020 were achieving the sale of my late parents' house, seven years after my dad died, and translating a novel by my sort-of-godson Niklas Maak. Some of you may remember his mother Karin, who came to Westonbirt for a week at the end of the summer term of 1968, as part of our very successful exchange. Another example of pure luck: we've been friends ever since. Her school in Hamburg-Harburg was where **Miss German Cooper** worked as a language assistant during her year abroad. Karin's friend Annegrit did an exchange with **Jenny Waterfield,** and **June Thompson** did one with Christi Müller. I don't think June and Christi were as compatible as we were. June hated swimming and Christi was extremely sporty. Karin told me recently that spending a week at a British boarding school was a hugely influential event at that stage in her life. Not just the immersion in English, although that was obviously important, but also the sense of community was a complete contrast to her own experience. She was an only child, both her parents worked full-time, and schools in Germany only operate from 08:00 to 13:00 so there are no shared institutional mealtimes. She even *liked* some of the school food, especially Cornish pasties!

Another memory about an international friendship is **Julia (Neath) Douglas**'s delightful exchange partner Laura. A few years after leaving school, I was on a summer course at the University of Stuttgart, chatting in German to a nice chap from Barcelona whose name escapes me. I said, "The only person I know who lives in Barcelona is called Laura Pla," and he said, "Laura is one of my lifelong best friends!" I wonder if Julia has kept in touch with her?

Penny Bysshe (Osborn) Well, I am still here! I did not realise how exhausted I was by my career as a dance teacher until we went into lockdown and I was forced to stop. While the world seemed to be falling apart around me the enforced rest and relaxation was actually just what I needed for the first few weeks.

My family has not been unaffected by the virus. Our son Simon caught it very early on, luckily only mildly. One of my nieces is now suffering very badly from post-Covid complications, and older relatives in poor health in Italy, confined to their apartment for over a year, caught it recently when venturing out to a hospital appointment. Simon has been filming since January in Prague, where the English variant is rife. We keep our fingers crossed for his safe return at the end of April. I fear we are not out of the woods yet.

I have found plenty of activities to keep me busy apart from Zoom calls. The garden has never been so manicured, but few were able to appreciate the results. During the first lockdown last year I carried on teaching ballroom and Latin over Zoom until the end of August. We spent all of September in France visiting English and French friends around the country, which was great fun and set us up for a long winter of lockdowns. On our return we carried on with Scottish dancing and have ended up teaching it over Zoom.

When winter came, I turned my attention to clearing out the house. It was long overdue as we have lived in the same house for over forty years. I also decided to improve my schoolgirl French and am now fluent in Duolingo. We formed a childcare bubble with our daughter Julia and her family, who live nearby, and this has been a great blessing.

Now things might be going to ease up, I am preparing to restart my ballroom and Latin classes, tea dances, and private dance lessons in June. I am wondering whether I really want to tie myself down so much. Time is limited and I really want to catch up on holidays missed. From now on my priority is spending time with my family and friends and my dance teaching will have to fit itself round our holidays rather than the other way round.

Deborah Dorrance-King (Dorrance) I missed our 2018 reunion as I had necrotising fasciitis from an insect bite picked up in Sudan. After some operations and skin grafts I am fine. I was able to go back to Sudan last spring, arriving back for lockdown. We were based near Meroe near the baby pyramids in Upper Egypt, with a rest day trip to Dongola, ending with our usual visits to the dialysis units in Khartoum. No more travelling afterwards. My husband died in June (not from Covid), but he managed to finish the paperwork for CE marking and FDA approval for his new vascular ultrasound machine that morning.

Charles is an architect in New York City, having just finished a project at the Smithsonian, and now working on a cosmetic start-up in San Francisco. He was able to work from London for three months after David died. Harry is at the Treasury and got married in August in Wimborne Minster; the party will be this August. Ralf is an artist, living at home. (Deborah, we all send *love and sympathy on the loss of your husband. CS)*

Julia Douglas (Neath) The most significant event of the past pandemic year has been the arrival of grandchild number five (Felix) born to our younger daughter Mia on 5th June last year. Fortunately for her he has proved an easy baby and she has stood up to the challenges of bringing him up in a rather lonely year spent padding round the parks of south east London with a couple of NCT friends in the same boat. Having been exposed to very few other children (or even adults), she has worried about him turning out to be socio-phobic, but as his granny I have been able to be part of her support bubble and I have seen little evidence of that so far!

The other piece of good news is that son Bruce and his partner Amanda, with their two young children, returned from Brazil to the UK to live in a rented house in London just prior to the first lockdown, which meant that they escaped the worst of the Brazilian virus. However, it has been a lonely time for them, too, as they have been unable to get to know people in their neighbourhood on account of the requirement to "stay at home and save the NHS". Fortunately, now just as the tide is turning, they are about to move into their own new house in Sydenham at the end of March, so let's hope that this will mean that they can start to make new friends and to settle in generally. Fred (7) is one of the many millions of kids who have missed out on a whole load of education, but fortunately appears quite bright so should catch up soon. His brother Josh is only just turning 2, so blissfully unaware of all this.

Our eldest, Laura, and her family have moved to a slightly larger house locally, in Oxted, and she has struggled manfully with the combined joys of homeschooling her two children (7 and 11) and working from home for three months.

Hubby John and I did try to play our part in the homeschooling of both seven-year-olds, using the internet and Zoom, to give their parents a break – the consequence of which is that we both now have a great deal of respect for the job that professional teachers do! Luckily, we have both been keeping well so far and have enjoyed many of the beautiful walks nearby.

Diana Gale (Forwood) In March last year the chairman of the tennis club I played at rang to say that the URC church had finally put their land up for sale and we would have to vacate the premises by 31st December. Would I be willing to be part of the Moving Ahead committee? And that was the main focus of my 2020. Luckily, there was a successful result after weeks of investigating different options, then negotiating the final contract. I've almost forgotten the endless difficulties of contacting people, fixing meetings with different council and private departments, only to find the main contact had been put on furlough – or worse. The weather let us down and we couldn't get the courts painted before the contractors stopped for the winter season, but it is now only eight days to go till the court gates open and the first games of tennis will be played at our new venue in Leatherhead. My kit is ironed and tennis shoes cleaned!

I did drive to Cambridge last September to visit a niece and family, otherwise I don't think I've been more than twelve miles from my home for a year. I've read, knitted, redecorated, gardened, Duolingo-ed, Zoomed, corresponded, especially with **Hilary Hughes (Moore)** who is still in Brisbane, and even baked a loaf of bread for the first time in my life! There's always something to do. What haven't I managed to achieve this year? De-clutter the attic. Oh! I was so pleased to see the photo of the WB lake – that really perked me up on a gloomy, grey day. All best wishes to everyone.

Alison Gauld (Taylor) I am so sorry to learn that Chris, too, has an autoimmune condition. I have had Sjogrens for about fourteen years now, and mine, too, deteriorated last winter. I guess it was bound to eventually. However, I have not let it stop me over the last year. I didn't send in any news last year as I was still grieving over my son Kristian, but since becoming Sacristan at St Peter's and Chairman of the Petersfield Voluntary Care Group there have been very worthwhile jobs to do which have kept me busy and spiritually fulfilled, as well as developing me as a person. So now I would say that I am at the happiest time of my life, despite having finally lost both parents, and my oldest son. I have learnt to cope with the grief and move on.

I am very fortunate in still having my husband, Jim, and my second son, Ashton. Ashton owns his own business, an executive search agency called Eton Bridge Partners in Windsor. They recruit CFOs, CEOs, and interim management for the top 200 FTSE companies. My four grandchildren are all doing well, and both granddaughters survived mild Covid last autumn.

During the first lockdown from April to July the number of our drivers decreased from about 40 to about seven. Most were over 70 and shielding. I had worked in recruitment in London, which helped. So, I embarked on a recruitment campaign and over the year I managed to find 26 new volunteers. You can imagine all the admin that was needed – DBS checks, references, checklists, documents, welcome packs, application forms, learning Zoom, etc. But then the number of patients needing volunteer drivers to take them to hospital dried up as the hospitals filled up with Covid patients. So, in order to keep them busy and to be useful I decided to offer our services to a local pharmacy to deliver their prescriptions to those who had registered with them for free prescription delivery. The NHS would normally have reimbursed the pharmacy for their costs, but we did it free. Over about a hundred days we delivered about 1500 prescriptions and still reimbursed our drivers for their expenses. All in all, we did 731 drives last year, and completely changed the PVCG. We became a registered charity, had a new logo, website and email address, and the average age of our drivers came down to represent a cross-section of the community, including some students. Recently I was invited to submit a report of our activities to the *Daily Mirror* for the June Campaign of 1000 Acts of Volunteering, and they said that it was just what they were looking for. I guess it is the old Westonbirt sense of duty that comes to the fore in times of crisis, and I feel sure that many of the old girls will have similar stories. The Very Rev Michael Clarke's sermons must have rubbed off on us, despite the antics we used to get up to in church on Sundays, one of which was passing a squeaking bat along the row without giggling! With lots of love to everybody.

Heather Hickman (Moffett) All in all, the past year has not been so bad for me. The first lockdown brought two of our children home for a few months – we all enjoyed being together much more than we could have imagined. The downside was not seeing my other son and grandsons (2 and 4) until we all managed to go to Cornwall for our usual annual holiday. Glenn and I were lucky to get away to Italy with friends in September, but a similar trip looks unlikely this year. It will be a treat just to go to London! I have missed seeing **Kate (McDowell)** and my sister **Ruth** there, and frequent theatre trips.

The big saviour for many of us has been the discovery of online bridge, which has been a mainstay of our lockdown social life, and kept us in touch with friends. I have been fortunate in that I am still working as a practice nurse a couple of days a week, which has got me out of the house and kept me pretty busy, including on vaccination clinics. Hopefully, life will be better by this time next year and we will be able to make up for lost time.

Judith Kramer (Nettleton) We have spent most of the year in Malaga where we had a hard lockdown in March last year for a couple of months. Fortunately we have a little dog so were able to go out for a walk a couple of times a day. Since then, we have been able to enjoy meeting friends outside the house, thanks to the climate!

Our son John, his wife and two children live in a nearby town so perimeter closures permitting we have been able to see them quite often. Our daughter Alice, husband and three children spent the month of July in Malaga, and we went back to Brussels for six weeks in early autumn. The hardest part of this difficult time has been not being able to see our son Andrew in Singapore. He had to cancel three planned trips to Europe, and we haven't seen him for about two years now. We were, however, fortunately able to see his two daughters (who live in the UK) when they spent the half term with us in February 2020. We are going back to Brussels at the beginning of April, and we shall stay for five weeks and – hopefully – get our vaccinations. We have the appointments, so fingers crossed.

I don't know if I mentioned that we had moved from our house with swimming pool etc and are now living in a seafront apartment in Malaga city. I love being able to walk to shops and living in a neighbourhood. We swam in the sea every morning from May until we went to Brussels! Last year was my 70th birthday and our 50th wedding anniversary. I celebrated my birthday in lockdown with Jim, and in Brussels we were able to go to one of our favourite restaurants for our anniversary. Sadly, it wasn't the get-together we had intended, but hopefully there will be other times for celebration. I can't believe our eldest granddaughter (the eldest of seven) will be 17 in May!

Chris Shaw (Morris) Thankfully, all our extended family (five children, three in-laws, imminently-to-be seven grandchildren) have stayed Covid-free and in employment, for which we must be grateful. Martin and I have mostly stayed in our village in North Yorkshire, where we have felt relatively safe, and have a lovely community of friends and neighbours. Unfortunately, the past year for me has been constrained by having contracted the autoimmune disease polymyalgia rheumatica, which combined with galloping osteoarthritis has proved painful, mobility limiting and extremely resistant to medication (steroids, thus giving me a chubby round face and making me immunosuppressed!)

However, on the plus side, I have, after a false start, found a dishy young award-winning rheumatologist, had what my son calls "a thorough MOT" and am on a new course of treatment, so things are slowly looking up. I can't really complain – it could be so much worse. Sadly, we are beginning to lose a number of friends and family for various reasons, and I have to remind myself that most of us are now in our seventies so it's inevitable that parts are wearing out and almost everybody is living with something. And I obviously haven't missed much over the past year! My 70th birthday came and went during lockdown without the hoped-for family gathering at February half term.

We squeezed in a holiday in sunny Lanzarote just before the first lockdown, but unfortunately had to cancel a trip to California for a family wedding in July. In all the circumstances we haven't had any trips away and hardly visited our house in Tetbury. We do know everything is alright there as it is currently occupied by my son Andrew, wife and two daughters (5 and 3) in between house moves.

My daughter Suzy, husband, and Ralph (7) and Nellie (2) have had a difficult year as they live in a boarding school in Sussex and have had to juggle the minefield of an ever-changing situation, not to mention ever-changing governmental edicts. They have all coped magnificently, but we long to see them again. My stepson Simon is a consultant at St Thomas's in London where it has obviously been all hands to the pump, and all the medics having crash retraining courses and multi-tasking. We are very proud of him, and of everyone involved.

Dee Sichel (Ferguson) We were extraordinarily lucky in being able to celebrate the births of two grandsons in 2020. Jack, Martha's brother, was born in May, and Zander, Charlie's first, in July. We managed to welcome Jack in the Coronation Gardens near their house in South London - magnums round a rug! Not seen him much as Christmas was cancelled, but we are hoping to see him in a few weeks' time and have erected a swing in anticipation.

We have been doing a big project with our orchard in the Isle of Wight. So lucky that it has given us something to do, the harvest and cider/juice making in the autumn, then pruning in early spring. We have also been building a huge barn to house a tractor. We have seen lots of Zander as they are renting a holiday home nearby, which is allowed because they are between houses, repeated house sales having fallen through.

I remain a safeguarding governor of Summerfields School, and like everyone else have been so impressed by the efforts staff have had to put in, particularly in the private sector. Let us hope we can move on from this spring to a better 2021. Best to all.

Jane White (Weston) Tom and I continue to live in Norfolk and if I had to choose anywhere to spend lockdown, I constantly remind myself how lucky we are to be here (beautiful walks on our doorstep, with the beach nearby) and have kept busy gardening, reading, and, having read the newsletter, my daughter even tempted me with two jigsaws. I had forgotten how addicted one could become and also how very rewarding and frustrating they are!

The one sadness has been no family gatherings and not seeing our twelve grandchildren. I was lucky enough to visit my daughter and family in Dubai in December, as soon as the lockdown finished. Sadly, she and her husband got Covid in February, which was not surprising after the huge numbers there for Christmas and New Year. My other daughter, Sarah, has been at home, having had a baby last July, but she took to home with enthusiasm and enjoyed the opportunity to have all the family together. My son has been kept busy working with Hopkins Homes in Suffolk and his two boys had wonderful online schooling, so all in all I feel we have been lucky.

We now look forward to the return of golf and tennis, which still plays a big part in my life…thanks to the Major Millman days! Then, hopefully, a trip to Dubai or California, where Tom's son and family live. Catching up with family is going to take some time!

Section 37 (1967)

Section Representative:
Jenifer Davidson (Moir)

Sultana Al-Quaiti (Rashid) Sooty has been stuck in Jeddah since 2019 and had to twice cancel her Friends of Hadhramaut fundraising event in Oslo in 2020 and 2021. It is now scheduled for May 2022: *www.hadhramaut.co.uk.*

Alison Boxley (Muir) I'm so pleased I decided to live in New Zealand where life is almost normal- compared to the rest of the world anyway. We are free to travel around New Zealand and I've been making the most of that freedom. The downside is that because our borders have been closed for nearly a year now, there is no travel outside NZ, even to Australia, and so I've not seen my daughters and granddaughter since Christmas 2019. Thank goodness for the internet.

The other sad news is that my younger brother, who lived in Corfu for the last 15 years, died suddenly from a stroke in February. A difficult time for the family as none of us could travel there and there remains much to sort out. A local woman has been a godsend arranging the funeral and doing all the official stuff.

Anne Collings (Watson) I am fine and have mostly enjoyed lockdown except for home schooling one of my grandchildren aged five. My youngest daughter, two boys and her husband live next door. Bryony and James both work full time so it seemed sensible for home schooling to be Grannie's duty. All I can say is I am glad my teaching career was secondary based!

I feel extremely lucky to live in the middle of nowhere, the nearest neighbours, apart from my daughter, are half a mile away. I enjoy fresh air and space and hardly ever meet anyone when I take my dogs for a walk. Lockdown must have been hell in a small flat in a big city.

Six years ago, I began making carved rocking horses and was able to get a couple of large horses finished during the first lockdown. I was very busy up until Christmas. The large horses take approximately 150 hours to complete. My workshop was incredibly cold and becoming increasingly wet with a leaky roof, so I have now taken over my conservatory, which is a far more pleasant workspace if a little unconventional. If anyone is interested in having a look, I have a Facebook page, Pitts Mill Rocking Horses.

I hope everyone has stayed Covid free and had the opportunity to be vaccinated. Let's hope that by the summer we will all be able to experience more normality.

Jenifer Davidson (Moir) Despite the restrictions, life has gone on much as usual over the past year. I am still doing a couple of days paid work a week, although I have given up one job with a local playgroup which I had done for 17 years. Have been playing lots of tennis (mostly singles from January to March) and going for walks. During the summer I explored parts of Edinburgh I'd never visited before. Amongst other things I walked the Water of Leith walkway from Balerno to Leith (about 13 miles, which I did in three stages), the canal from Fountainbridge to Westerhailes (still have more of that to do), and Silverknowes to Cramond along the shores of the Forth. More locally we were free to roam on Prestonfield Golf Course and of course Holyrood Park is close by.

Rebecca and Ewen are doing OK in Stonehaven. Rebecca is able to work from home, and Ewen has been at the restaurant, although with the latest restrictions it is currently closed. Fortunately, the fish and chip shop part is able to function fairly normally and has been very busy, and he also takes the van out a couple of days a week. They keep exercised by two large golden retrievers.

Have missed going to church but am still active as treasurer. The lockdown has impacted considerably on our income since the church has been closed to visitors and we have not been able to hold weddings, concerts etc.

It was inevitable under the circumstances that our planned reunion for June 2020 at Sooty's in London had to be cancelled. We are now planning a reunion for September 2021 based at the Hare & Hounds. So far there has been a good response and numbers are growing.

Hilary Davis (Stone) I was very interested to read about the restoration of the lake at Westonbirt, as I have many happy memories of walking around the grounds, and I look forward to seeing it once we are allowed to visit again. I have very little to report this year: Andrew and I have been walking in the beautiful, wooded parts of Ledbury and exploring other areas in the locality.

Apart from that, I have been enjoying various activities via Zoom, especially the yoga classes. We have everything we need to keep going during the lockdowns but, like everyone else, we can't wait to be able to see our family again, in particular, our grandson, Lewis, who is now two years old.

Jenny Groom (Brooke) Hell's bells – I was 70 last birthday which means everyone in this Section is about that age too! No idea where the last 50 years have gone. My career really started in my mid-twenties when I was employed by a wonderful person called Rosamunde Bern who ran a travel PR company. I was her first employee. Working with Rosamunde was a wonderful apprenticeship, and I took to PR like a duck to water. It was the early days, quite male dominated but huge fun and, of course, I did a fair bit of travelling throughout Europe.

I moved on to consumer PR working with an agency whose main client was Boots the Chemist. I then married and after having my first child left that agency and worked freelance while Camilla and my son, Pelham, were growing up.

In my 50s, after an earlier move to Wiltshire for my husband's work when I ran a cookery school for children for a while, I was invited to handle the PR for Bonne Maman conserves and compotes and subsequently took on the PR and marketing of Bonne Maman biscuits, cakes, and chilled desserts – the entire gamut of the brand's products in the UK. I stayed with them until my early 60s, looking after some other clients as well; chocolate and wine (not bad!)

I'm now retired, have recently downsized to a house in Calne, help run the Devizes Food & Drink Festival, and became a first-time grandmother in March last year, which means I've hardly seen my granddaughter and not had much opportunity to become a spoiling granny. Looking forward to that changing soon. Of course, I'd love to see/be contacted by/catch up with anyone from my era. *(Ed. Due to data protection please contact your Section Rep if you would like details of how to contact other section members.)*

Hope that gives an overview of the past millions of years!

Christine Maclaren My garden had never looked so tidy as it did by last August, and I have walked miles every day (one of the benefits of living in a rural area). But I have to admit I have learnt no new skills and I am no better at cooking/baking now than I was before! There isn't even much point in turning out cupboards and loft spaces as there aren't any charity shops to send stuff to.

We managed a holiday before lockdown last year to Vietnam, Cambodia, and Laos, but then postponed two holidays, one of which has now been postponed again. Like many people, I haven't see my son since Christmas 2019, and vaccinations are being rolled out so slowly in Belgium I suspect we might not see him until next year now. At least we have Skype and Zoom!

Sue Pasfield (Ross) To our amazement we do have some news in this Covid year – we managed to sell/pass on our business to a larger firm which is proving a very satisfactory outcome for me, my hubby (trusty but not awfully-enjoying-it finance director) and the team. I got involved in online learning some 40 years ago and it's proved an interesting and mostly fulfilling career, during which I worked in Brussels, Paris, a bit in Spain and a lot in USA, always trying to change how teaching and training is conducted. Something I've been trying to change and influence all these years is finally being accelerated thanks to lockdown.

Jeni Whittaker (Waterfield) My news in this year could have been pretty bleak, but I won't go into the horriblenesses - we've all had those. Good news is that my novel about my suffragette great-aunt is finally seeing the light of day in two or three months' time. It's called *The Courage Game* by Jeni Whittaker. I thought about writing this one under my maiden name, because family members feature, but decided to retain the name I've had for nearly fifty years, since that's what most people know me by. When I know the ISBN number, I'll let you know. *(Ed: It's 978-1800464513 and it will be published on 21st September 2021).* For those who are interested, it's not just about the suffragettes, though that is the central part of the story - it's also a story about love and loss, families and, particularly, sisterhood. You will know that I've been writing drama resources (47 of them now!) for drama teachers for the last twenty or so years under the name of Dramaworks. I shall keep that going for another two or three years, but at seventy am thinking about closing shop finally and concentrating more on fiction.

Section 36 (1966)

Section Representative:
Julia Braggins (Cock)

Moi Beveridge (Anderson) What a horrendous year - at times I don't think I've ever been so glum. Appalling three years anyway, mainly because the roosts I plumped for were not remotely suitable (my flat in London, and then this morgue). My fault, I was so desperate to find somewhere I didn't do my research. Never buy in a block which says over-sixties - they're nearly all over 80 and it's dire. I've called it death's waiting room. In its favour, it's warm and tidy, but the occupants are of a totally different background (trying not to be snobby but failing). Luckily, thanks to my father, I had managed to squirrel away some cash and kicked on and found a 'forever' home which never came on the market. In a largish village opposite a pub, with a Chinese, deli etc very close. Says it's 1841 but I reckon it's circa 1650 - good rooms and 'perfick' for me. Not sold this yet, and shall take a fat loss, but I can't take it with me so *tant pis*. Almost ready and just waiting for an electric Aga and carpets. Finally cracked it - phew!

What a pig of a year, and don't think Boris *et al* can cover themselves in glory. They were so lucky to be saved by the advent of the vaccine and the efficient roll-out. On a different note, **Poi's** husband's second wife is divorcing him. Sad thing is he has a number of family things I should like back, but a fat lot of chance in that direction. About the last time I saw her when she was vaguely lucid, she offered me a lot of my mother's jewellery and I didn't take it as didn't want to deprive her.

Julia Braggins (Cock) This time last year we were in sunny Spain, listening to stories of a strange new virus afflicting the passengers of a cruise liner. Little did we know what was to come. In fact, what came for us, rather soon after our flight home, was what I'm sure was a dose of Covid for us both, but who knows since no-one was getting tested except those in hospital. We just put it down to aeroplane flu. Since then, we've been marking time, fortunately able to see families over the summer, but otherwise getting on with huge amounts of sorting out, and enjoying walks in this lovely part of Kent.

This year I've been in touch with lots of WB contemporaries: **Ronnie Boswell** from Florida, **Jo Clarke (Brooke)** who now lives quite close by in Kent, **Val Cassidy (Simpson)** who has just moved house in Dunoon, **Sandy Marshall (Hellawell)** and **Judy Turner (Marryat).** At least the lockdown has provided both the time and incentive for staying connected. And it is so lovely to hear from everyone who takes the trouble to write in with their news. Thank you!

Fiona Chilton (Forsyth) What a year. Extraordinary times to live through. We feel so lucky to be in lovely Hampshire countryside during this pandemic. Have taken up knitting after many years, and the family now all have fun coloured socks! Have found out so much about dyeing wool and different sheep. Most of the family are in Devon, so I read to my grandsons on WhatsApp but can't wait to meet up with them all when allowed. Youngest son stuck working in Singapore, so 18 months since we've seen him. Still working as a counsellor for Naomi House Children's Hospice, all online or phone, so very different. Longing to get back on the tennis court and also to the choir, but get exercise walking the dog and gardening. Roll on the rest of the year and hopefully freedom again.

Sarah Ferguson In early February last year I flew from New Zealand to Japan for ski-touring and powder-skiing with good friends. By then there was evidence of a "bad flu" virus, and we were prepared with our face-masks and hand-sanitiser. I returned from NZ to UK on 11th March to self-isolate having managed a supermarket delivery to arrive at the same time.

By then it was becoming a serious issue and I didn't want to be part of the problem. The actual lockdown was the most extraordinary, wonderful time. Our village reminded me of the Sixties with few cars and visitors. I thoroughly enjoyed my solitude and new greenhouse. Thankfully, my favourite yoga teacher started Zoom classes, and having thought I would not receive his teaching during the year I have been blessed with four two-hour classes each week. This winter's lockdown has been a surprise. My first winter in UK for 47 years. I am Nordic walking for at least five miles a day and have discovered many hidden delights and found new paths. I receive my first vaccination tomorrow for which I am very grateful.

Lucy Fisher (Sadleir) Strange times and I can't imagine life ever being the same again as we've all wound down so much. We managed to have a week in a lovely cottage in South Wales in September and left the day before they locked down. Also managed to have daughter, Zoe, and family for Christmas which was wonderful. My son Tim and family are returning in the summer, after five years in Sweden, to live in Devon. Last July we all went there for a weekend to see the barn they are buying which was a highlight. These long separations are awful, especially when the littlest grandchild (a darling girl) is only two. I can't wait to have them back!

Veronique Lewis (Hall) We have managed to stay Covid-free, had the jab, and are longing to see the family again. Luckily no-one can come to stay yet as the spare room is full of bags of stuff from a clear out, that can't be taken anywhere yet. Roll on spring when I can get into the garden again.

Sandy Marshall (Hellawell) The request for news came with a picture of the school in the snow: it took me back to February 1963, Lower Vth, Dorchester, freezing dorms, lax pitches under deep snow, they were unusable for half a term. It did get quite boring going for walks instead - crocodiles, grey macs, but for the non-sporty, like me, it had its compensations. We were allowed to have boots sent from home – I had those zipped furry-lined ones that came to just over your ankle. The water was hot, though – memories of red carbolic soap and trying to warm one's hands in the cloakroom we shared with Badminton...

Now, in February 2021, everyone is realising that it's been nearly a year since the first lockdown. The last concert given by Gloucester Choral in the cathedral was on 14th March – Bach's St John Passion. It was a moving performance in the circumstances, as we realised that would probably be the last for some time.

Thereafter it's been a world of Zoom, having a go at sourdough, reading books long ignored on the shelves, and finding local paths that we had not realised were there. We did get to Scotland in that lovely spell of weather in August – warm enough to go in the sea, and none of this wetsuit stuff! A few nights in Devon in the autumn, but our camper has been very underused. It's all been easier for us, though, than for those with families and jobs to go to – we just hope that as the seasons turn, things will ease for everyone.

Karen Olsen What a strange time we are in at the moment. We thought it would all be over by last summer and did not expect to be locked down again for the third time. I am sure we are all experiencing similar problems but as long as everyone is managing to keep well that is the best news. Have had the first dose of vaccine now, as most of us more mature members have, and looking forward to the second dose in May.

Otherwise, I am doing my Pilates classes on Zoom plus an art history course with the U3A. I have bubbled with part of my family, so at least we can get together some of the time. I miss the grandchildren. They are too young to really understand, but we do drive-bys and Facetime, and try to see them on a walk at a suitable social distance. They are both thriving at home with their mother giving them so much help and attention. Joshua's reading is exceptionally good for his age, so I do not think lockdown has held him back.

Last summer we all spent a lot of time in my garden, as it can be accessed via a gate without going through the house, so picnics, games and a lot of laughter were the order of the day. Still running our family business, which has not been easy during Covid, and have done fewer visits but more phone calls and emails. Some of our tenants had to have a helping hand as during the first lockdown their businesses were hugely impacted. Hope we can get back to some sort of normal life in the not-too-distant future.

Alison Palmer (Wheeler) Well, nearly a year since lockdown happened. I am here in my lovely house that Mick and I were intending to downsize into, but sadly he died before it was ready. So, I am happily settled in now and have been here for 2 years. I am surprisingly OK with lockdown. I walk most days with a friend, so get friendship and exercise. I think I am getting lazier.

Last summer was good, when we could be outside and have six people to entertain in the garden. I had a number of lunch parties.

We were released last time just before my mid-June birthday, and my nephew was married virtually that day, so I spent it with one of my sons by their pool, watching the wedding online. We had a chat-room reception afterwards. Brilliant.

My new granddaughter Beatrice was born mid-July. I have kept up with her progress on videos and she has grown up playing to camera as she is so photographed. Lots of Facetime calls to me and her other grandparents, who live in Brussels and haven't seen her in person yet. Luckily, I have, as I bubble with them and go and stay. Her siblings, aged 14 and 10, adore her and she them. WhatsApp groups have been good too. I have one with my Westonbirt year, amongst others, so keep in touch and waste time with all the videos being sent around.

I have discovered a website called *www.virtualtrips.io* which takes you to places like Florence, Venice, and Rome, and I am going to Budapest on Friday. No cost, but you are asked to tip the guide. I have taken up re-caning chairs. I started at my upholstery class when it was still running this time last year, and have continued at home finishing one for Carolyn, then a chair and a wonderful pew for my son. I am now open to recaning chairs for others as a small business, as am well practised! I have had one enquiry, and need to spread the word.

Alison Parry (Sturdy-Morton) It's been a strange year for the whole world with so many ups and downs for everyone. To some extent I have enjoyed isolation in my tiny Barbican flat. At the start of lockdown, I read *A Journal of the Plague Year* by Daniel Defoe (irony intended) as I'm a few streets away from where he lived and wrote it, making his writings seem very real and of the moment. Am pretty sure the City of London just looked up what they did in 1665 and used the template. They removed all benches and the police patrolled, including private gardens, to make sure people socially distanced and when outside only exercised. I had disturbing dreams of my childhood in the civil war in Beirut... long-hidden memories that I had to work through. Not a totally happy time.

On the plus side my daughter, teaching from home in France, asked the school if I could be her classroom assistant. They used Discord and students were not visible, but could both write and speak at the same time. I had fun correcting the fast-flowing written English and did the exercises and quizzes with everyone, so definitely improved my French! This was, of course, a clever ruse of my daughter's to make sure I checked into school every day. It was also an interesting insight into how families managed and shared.

The wonders of the internet made the world a much smaller place while we are unable to travel. My son and daughter-in-law had their first child, at the height of the pandemic, in New York City. The birth was complicated, and Alexander ended up in NICU for a few days.

All very worrying, but at least we could keep in touch through technology. He is now happy, healthy, and gearing himself up to walk. I may have missed out on cuddles with my grandson but get daily photos or videos and amazingly was on a family Zoom session when he made his first attempt at crawling. Zoom has been a boon and made life seriously enjoyable as well as pan-continental. I miss hugging my family and friends, especially as the past year has been the first in my life where I have been totally alone for Easter, Christmas, New Year, and my birthday. However, with WhatsApp and Zoom, those family days were happy and celebrated with long distance contacts.

Have avoided all the baking fads but am quite pleased with my hair cutting efforts, and my hair is shorter now than after my last professional haircut a year ago! I really miss live theatre and concerts but have made every effort to support a lot of on-line events, discussions, shows and helping people where possible. I also took advantage of being able to walk to several museums when they opened in the autumn and, with the booking system, enjoyed the quiet visits - one benefit of living in the concrete jungle!

Tilly Roberts de Zagal (Roberts) I have been living outside of Santiago since December 2019. I have a small property in El Cajón del Maipo, approximately 50km east of the capital. Village life suits me. My upbringing was in the Cheshire countryside. Westonbirt provided so much of beautiful rurality with many delightful hamlets in the neighbourhood. Hence, in many ways, my lifestyle is similar. Chile was badly hit by Covid in May 2020. At present (Feb 2021) numbers are lower but not low enough for proper tracing. As in other countries, the population is undergoing vaccination procedures. My turn is this week.

On the night of Saturday Jan 30th, 2021, our little village of San Alfonso suffered major landslides in three areas. Approximately one third of the homes were either swept away or filled with mud and rocks. Chileans are used to emergencies caused by nature and evacuation procedures resulted in no deaths. We were without water, electricity, or communication for two days.

My little house was unaffected, but the surrounding driveway and garden were loaded with about 3cm of mud. The mud has hardened and cracked into pieces of about 10-15 cm wide. I've had a lot of discussion as to whether I should leave as is, punch holes in it or turn it back in. The main agreement is that the mud is good for the garden (we are approaching autumn) and to avoid turning it as that would release carbon into the atmosphere to produce CO^2. Remember our chemistry classes?

I am on the village board of directors for our canal and ditch-watering system. The whole 4km of channels was covered by approximately 3-6m of mud, rocks, trees etc. A disaster, especially as small farmsteads need the water for their fruit and nut crops. Also, some homes have no fresh water access. A young member of the community who is well known on social networks put in a request for help. Two days ago, I transported 100 roast chicken and rice lunches up the mountainside to young volunteers who arrived with shovels, pickaxes, and helmets, to work all day cleaning out about 600m of channel. This has entirely renewed my faith in our young people. A group of fishermen from Coronel down south sent a refrigerated truck with enough fresh fish for the whole village to enjoy. A group of volunteers from Santiago have cooked lunch every day at the school for anyone needing it. The list could go on much longer.

You may have heard of Project Trust based on the Isle of Col in Scotland. For about 20 years, I have been working with young people in their gap year, who are selected to serve for one year under reasonable hardship conditions. Many have been placed under my tutorship in the school here where I have worked voluntarily for the last seven years. They have now got together online and formed a fundraiser on Gofundme.com. Wonderful! Incidentally, I thoroughly recommend this organisation for any WB leavers who want to take a gap year that may well change their lives in a positive way.

Section 35 (1965)

Section Representative:
Marilyn Jones (Bird)

No news returned this year

Section 34 (1964)

Section Representative:
Julia Popham (Bishop)

Ann Beattie (Buckland) What a very strange year 2020 was, and now at the end of this month it will be a year of lockdown. As the first one started I was very surprised to find I was considered clinically vulnerable because I take immune suppressive drugs, as I was diagnosed with autoimmune hepatitis many years ago. This had never caused me any problems during my nursing career. So not going out for twelve weeks came as quite a shock. Once we were allowed more freedom we didn't go anywhere apart from visiting friends in Dorset for a few days. I felt we would be ok with them.

Our small garden and being near the coast helped to keep us sane. We have kept in touch with friends on Facebook etc. Soon this current lockdown will ease, and it will stop feeling like Groundhog Day every day. John and I have both had our first vaccines with no ill effects and hope to have the second ones in April. We are looking forward with hope for better times as this year heads towards summer.

Clare Carter (Binney) Like most people, I imagine, news seems scant this year. I was shielding from March onwards, grocery deliveries and the like worked fine with a mixture of online orders and kind friends but I did find not being able to go outside the garden, even just for exercise, very trying, but that's been lifted since the summer.

The garden did get much more attention than it's used to, I'm not sure it looked any better, but I felt good to have something to do outside. When the length of the disruption became apparent, my U3A got very into doing things by Zoom, committee meetings of course but now a big range of activities, quizzes, garden group meetings, ukulele practice and many more. We even had a Zoom Christmas party and are now having coffee mornings. It helps to keep in touch with people. One of the joys of recent months has been a Study One link up over Zoom. **Claire Marshall, June Cohen** and I have been meeting virtually every couple of months and putting the world to rights, plus reminiscing about life when we were at WB.

Looking forward, I have had my first jab so feel a little bit more confident about going to essential places. Here in Northern Ireland, we have a series of steps laid out for coming out of lockdown but no dates. I think the first easing will be after Easter, and we have five steps to go. I have no idea when I will see the family again. They are all well, the grandsons growing up fast, but we can none of us travel at the moment and they have no idea when they will get vaccinations. Neither Japan nor Denmark have had the terrible number of deaths that we've had. Azuma missed a little school early on but has been there since the summer, and Helen and Kristian have been working from home but, fortunately, Finn has been able to go to nursery most of the time. Not much can be done with him about, he's an active chatterbox now, happy to talk over Zoom - he cooks for me in his toy kitchen. Last time it was cake and broccoli (spelling of latter not good!)

Mary Cave (Rawlence) Mary's elder sister **Elizabeth Ells (Rawlence)** who lives in Canada, has sent in this interesting story which was recently told to Elizabeth by Mary, whose memory was triggered by the news of the restoration of the lake to its early glory.

"There was still a lake when I was at Westonbirt. One winter it was exceptionally cold, and the lake froze very solidly; so solidly that skating was allowed on the lake. Since the lake was small, girls were allocated half hour at a time in order that everyone had a turn. Indeed, the winter was so cold, and the cold so prolonged, that a local gravel pit also froze and one Saturday the school took those who wished to go, to the gravel pit to skate."

June Cohen (Kefford) I think that I have spent this year in many varying ways, like so very many of my age and generation. It has been a year when we have all had to deal with several different kinds and degrees of loss and challenge. We have all had to embrace new terms in our vocabulary like Zoom; words like bubble, lockdown and tier have all adopted completely new meanings. I have been incredibly fortunate. I have kept my health, physical and mental, due in no small part to the love and kindness of family and friends.

I have finally realised the one thing that my time at Westonbirt prepared me for in this crazy year, and that is that rain, gales and cold are to be endured, nay even enjoyed, with fortitude and a positive attitude, which, during this past year we have all needed in order to have any sort of social life at all!

I have Zoomed with both new friends and old friends, the latter category includes some wonderful exchanges with **Claire Marshall, Clare Carter (Binney), Helen Faircliffe (Weinholt)** and **Anne Grocock**.

I have Zoomed with my choir, with church, conducted interviews and played games and done quizzes with the family. I have had lovely phone conversations, which have included chats with **Carol Brawn (Topham)** and **Jo Wilson (Forcey),** and wonderful email exchanges with **Deni Bittolo (Porter)** and a visit from **Sue Coveney (Hyman)** in the summer – with whom I have even swapped our ridiculous autograph book entries from 1958! I have "climbed Everest" on a cross trainer and actually climbed Brown Willy in Cornwall with a friend, on probably the worst day of weather in the whole of last autumn.

I have spent more time gardening than ever before and have walked miles, mostly on our lovely beaches, with friends, as we have shouted our conversations at the approved distance, both from each other and from others.

My middle son came back on unpaid leave from abroad to keep his old mum company for seven weeks in the first lockdown, despite my initial protestations, but that was a real tonic. I have been lucky enough to have seen the rest of my family, during the summer and at other odd outdoor times, and I bubble with my lovely daughter and her family, who live fairly close by. My eldest granddaughter was 21, this last week. Where have the years gone?!

Pippa Dutton (Thomson) Lockdown again has made us aware of our age. My husband is 85 going on 60 and we have been very law abiding and isolated as instructed, but we have not succumbed to online deliveries and have still managed to shop.

We were fortunate to squeeze in a two-week holiday in Turkey in September, but are doubtful that the trips booked in all good faith for May this year will happen, as they involve air travel. How lucky we are to have a house, a small garden in which we can sit, and to be retired so not in danger of losing our jobs. Dickie and I get on so well with one another that we have enjoyed the time under house arrest, although we are missing our friends and family very much and looking forward to getting back to all the things which London has to offer, of which we have been deprived, as well as our club, Hurlingham, where my husband plays a lot of croquet.

The telephone has been a bonus, as have emails, but I don't enjoy Zoom, so have avoided it as much as possible. An exception has had to be made for meetings with my livery company, the Musicians Company, who have been doing valiant work helping young freelance musicians survive by promoting lunchtime concerts on You Tube. As for singing, my main hobby, the sound is just not the same standing on the drawing room carpet singing to a computer, so I don't. Oh, to get back to live singing! My last concert was mid-March 2020.

One happy outcome of lockdown has been catching up with old friends not seen or heard of for years, and cycling round London on the almost deserted streets. One day we cycled round the City to find it a ghost town, with deserted and boarded up buildings; the only people around being in high viz jackets and helmets, either demolishing or building. It was also interesting to cycle round the attractive back streets of Kensington, Chelsea and Victoria, where in mid-February there were still Christmas wreaths on some doors. So many of the lovely primary homes are empty, their owners having retreated to second homes elsewhere - and who can blame them?

Charlotte Essex (Humpidge) Well, what a year! But things are improving with the vaccinations. Do so hope everyone is OK, even though it's been a difficult time for all of us, not seeing family and friends. Richard has been given the all-clear as regards his cancer treatment - such a blessing - and an intense course of physiotherapy for his knee injury has helped and it's now slowly improving.

Our greatest joy is that Jonathan and Gail have just adopted an eight-year-old child. She is adorable, full of energy and has settled remarkably well. Sadly, we have seen very little of Zofia, now 9, nor Catherine who's been self-isolating in London since the first lockdown. Andrew has been lucky enough to work the entire time with his job for a property management company. Our large garden has been a great benefit, numerous jobs have been tackled, and paperwork and general clutter etc. cleared out. We've never had so much free time with no antique fairs and few commitments.

Susan Fisher (Barritt) 2020 was a year to forget! We managed a few days in Portugal just before the first lockdown and then everything was cancelled. Whilst I do appreciate that the last 12 months have been unbearable for many people, (our daughter has found it hard being a single mother of a 14-year-old adopted son at home for much of the year) it has not really been that bad for us. Living by the sea, we have space to walk, and the view is always changing, so even in lockdown life has not been too bad; but we are looking forward to being able to get out and about a bit further afield. I'm hoping we will be able to celebrate our Golden Wedding in some style in August.

Ann Grocock What a year we have had! Lockdown after lockdown and seemingly at some point no end to it, and away from friends and family. But there have been some bright spots and things do look a lot better for the future.

What would we have done without Zoom? Bill had to stop going into his laboratory in March, but the coffee morning meetings continued once a week on Zoom, which kept us up to date with what was, and is, going on in the university. We were often joined by graduate students and it was good to get their thoughts on things.

Bill had his 90th birthday in November, and there had been plans for great celebrations, which obviously had to be curtailed, but it is amazing what you can do with Zoom and Kudoboard. *(Ed: I had to look this up, too... a virtual bulletin board of messages, gifs (animated images), and photos for remote celebrations, apparently!)* We had a session run from the lab with people logging into Zoom from all over the world, and video birthday wishes from as far away as Mexico and Japan. We had a grand family Zoom session too, so all was well.

In spite of the lockdowns, I have still been involved with the Nuffield Oxford Hospitals Fund, which I will step down from as chair in May. It has been quite moving to hear about how the medical profession has been managing during the pandemic and in particular how the medical students have been affected. Many have actually been involved on the front line. The good parts have been being able to be in touch with family and friends by Zoom - we last saw Bill's grandchildren in the flesh last summer and so are hoping to see them all again before too long.

I have enjoyed seeing **Claire Marshall, June Cohen, and Helen Faircliff** on two Zoom sessions recently, and I am hoping at some point again we shall meet in person. And I hear regularly from **Chris Bryan** who is currently in Florida, and at the time of writing this I think is still waiting for her vaccination. Much has been made of the Oxford vaccine and we sat in on a webinar the other day with Sir John Bell, Regis Professor of Medicine, talking about how Oxford got ahead of the game with the vaccine with the team at the Jenner Institute here. Interesting, but a bit scary as one realises how many potential worldwide pandemics there have been in the last twenty or so years (SARS, MERS etc.) and that there are likely to be more to come. Hopefully, we will have learned enough from this one to cope with the next one. It will be interesting to see what the G7 discussions come up with.

Looking forward to 2022 and a bit of normality!

Claire Marshall My heart goes out to those who have themselves, or who are close to those, who have suffered physically or mentally in the clutches of the pandemic. I give thanks that my family remains unscathed though isolation takes a toll. Like others, there were many cancellations: a choral trip to Prague & Vienna, a fortnight in Hungary, followed by two weeks in

Mongolia; dozens of concerts; singing with my choir; and a dearth of coffee chats with friends.

Outweighing all this is much good news. My daughter and her family moved to the Ottawa area in September and are now only 50 miles down the road, not a thousand. It has been a joy to visit whenever I wish as singletons may bubble with a family. And that family is slated to grow in the late summer of 2021 with a second grandchild.

Fortunate, too, has been the discovery of Zoom, which now connects me to several small clusters of WB chums; to a welter of friends and heretofore little-known cousins spanning the globe; and to an unexpectedly lively online program with my choir (lots of singing, though unheard, of course!)

My time with OrKidstra ended in November (after nine and a half years on the Board, six as Chair) and I am looking around for new challenges within the world of community service. As always, there is no lack of those!

Rosemary O'Malley (Matthews) I looked at the photographs of the lake with real pleasure. I never saw it in its demise and think I would have been very depressed to have done so. I hope that giant sequoia tree is still standing proud on the way down to the lake?

We have been fine during this lockdown . This is where we are very lucky to live out in Ceredigion. We have the country around us and the basic shops in Lampeter itself. We still have the two whippets, so I go out every day to walk them.

The garden has been my big thing over the last year. I have pruned everything to within an inch of its life and set up another raised veg bed. A very old prunus tree had to come down, and for a long time I just couldn't get anyone to come and do it with a chain saw; so, I bought a very hefty branch lopper and also a very sharp pruning saw and set to work. Only trouble is the arthritis in the back is a bit of a hindrance, and I would come away from my task bent over like one of those old gardeners in those black and white Victorian photos, but there is nothing like a challenge to keep one fit to the best of one's ability. I also went back to baking all our own bread and particularly enjoyed making focaccia and Italian country bread and baguettes. When the weather was awful, I set upon the cellar and Brendan's library, and managed to do quite a good clear-out, which traumatised him at the time, but when I had finished he admitted that it all actually looks very nice!

Does anyone know a place where we might be able to sell very old books without ISBN numbers? Most are religious or certainly literary.

Some members of our family got Covid but were not too badly affected: our son was working out in Kabul and was not able to get back home for about five months. All his team got Covid out there but were ok. Our son-in-law is a policeman up in Newcastle and he got it too; but he was ok after a few days. So, we have been very fortunate.

Julia Popham (Bishop) An enormous thank you to everybody who responded to me with their news this year. We really have a bumper crop and that is brilliant. Very many thanks to you all, I am extremely grateful.

Nigel and I feel very fortunate to live here with a good-sized garden and very easy access to Wimbledon Common and near to Richmond Park too. So many Londoners were trapped in tower blocks with very little access to green spaces. We are just so grateful to have come through the pandemic, so far unscathed, but are fully aware that this is not the case for very many people.

Like everybody else we have really missed seeing our friends and family, but we have done lots of quizzes with them, the local Arts Society has provided us with loads of very interesting lectures, we've been on Zoom virtual walks of Wimbledon Village and the Common, and in March I helped to organise a charity art history webinar on William Morris in aid of Cancer Research UK (CRUK) which raised £6,000. We celebrated Easter yesterday in our local church and it was so very special to be able to be there again with our friends, even if socially distanced.

I have been in touch with **Joyce Seaman, Lella Fountaine, Sian King** and **Pippa Dutton**. I understand that **Jo Wilson (Forcey)** is currently in South Africa and has been in touch with **Lella Fountaine**. Recently it was really good to have a long telephone call from **Mary Cave (Rawlence)** and we happily reminisced on various subjects ranging from Hades to hair-washing and debugging, and finally how we were only allowed to phone home on the most rare of occasions.

Alannah Rylands (Hall) Absolutely nothing has happened this year. Luckily, we live in the middle of the country with a large garden and plenty of space to walk and the sea isn't that far away. Children and grandchildren live in the south, so we haven't seen them for months. We had hoped to get together for Easter, but that has fallen by the wayside.

I think I shall be a plump alcoholic by the end of this! Husband longing to get his old cars back on the road and be able to go on old car trips with like- minded friends. The trouble is, when we reach this age we don't have the years to lose. At the moment it is difficult to remember which week it is, let alone what day of the week!

Joyce Seaman (Carnegie) My first hope is that nobody reading this has lost family members or close friends during the past year. It has been such a hard year for so many. We have felt very fortunate being able to work at home with minimal disruption. We finally moved at the beginning of November into the house we have been building in Oxford. We shared it with the builders until Christmas Eve when they finally finished most things.

Our son, who lives in New York, was married in July, having had to cancel his original wedding plans for June. We attended on Zoom and the whole very simple service was rather lovely, and was, of course, far less of a performance than the planned wedding.

My husband, Tom is due to retire in September, but I shall carry on at the Ashmolean until I am no longer useful.

Section 33 (1963)

Section Representative:
Helen Faircliff (Wienholt)

Ros Barham (Jakeman) What a year! I guess we have all found it quite challenging. The first lockdown had a strange element of novelty about it. The lack of noise from traffic and overhead planes seemed to make nature come into its own and I was more aware of the beautiful bird song around us. Taking the dog for his daily walk was a great therapy but also surreal with no cars to wait for, no pedestrians, just the occasional runner to step aside for. Thanks to the wonderfully warm spring I was able to spend lots of time in the garden doing some long overdue maintenance.

For the second year running, our holiday was cancelled. 2019 was thanks to Thomas Cook going into liquidation two days before our flight, and 2020 the announcement of lockdown!

I think the thing I have missed most is seeing the family. What a blessing Zoom has been. However, our youngest daughter was compelled to work from home so spent the first three months in solitary confinement. Once we were allowed to bubble she moved back in with us and has been an absolute treasure, not least insisting on doing the weekly shop as my husband is in the vulnerable category.

I have just spent a week in hospital, (thankfully not Covid-related), and seen first-hand what a wonderful job our nursing staff are doing and the difficulties they are up against with many of the patients presenting with mental health issues.

Having spent the last 22 years of my working life with the Prison Service, I can begin to appreciate what a custodial sentence is like!

Suzanne Burroughs (Bradbury) Thank goodness for my garden. I have been growing as many vegetables as possible to give to family and friends.

I was able to play croquet during lockdown, but it doesn't take place at our club during the winter. I am hoping that lockdown may ease and that we might be able to start again in March providing the lawns are useable.

I am also lucky to be able to play bridge with my clubs online, which helps pass the evenings as I do not find TV very exciting. My main social life is my regular local walking where I come across regular dog walkers and we are able to exchange pleasantries! All the rain has made the ground very slippery, and one has to choose walks with care!

But I am so lucky to have space.

Sue Coveney (Hyman) In September 2020, on our way back from a few days in Cornwall, we visited **June Cohen (Kefford)** and sat in the garden of her wonderful seaside house in Teignmouth, Devon. June is a busy grandmother and also looks so well and young, especially from daily sea swimming in the summer.

Later in September Michael (husband) and I visited **Caroline Henderson (Beloe)** and Nick Henderson for a delicious lunch in their impressive garden in Putney. We walked quite a lot of the way. I noticed many late summer wildflowers around Barnes and the Wetland Centre.

I have been in touch with **Alannah Watson Hall (Rylands)**. Not only is she a gifted gardener and cook, but she is also now breadmaking, and has started again to make a beautiful tapestry seat cover. How she cooked so many meals for all the grandchildren and family in August at their seaside house is a miracle.

I am looking forward to meeting up with **Helen Faircliff (Wienholt)** once Kew Gardens open up their cafés again. I love being a volunteer at Kew and we hope to return after Easter.

We now have a five-month-old gorgeous grandson. I had given away all baby accoutremonts so will have to search for new ones. Our granddaughters, age 9 and 7, are happy to have returned to school. During lockdown they have become very attentive older sisters.

We are hoping to visit **Dominique Goy Blanquet** in Paris later this year. She taught French at Westonbirt in 1964.

Liz Davies (Edwards) Life this year has been quiet and uneventful but without illness. We have stayed at home reading, doing jigsaws, sudokus and Zooms and being really grateful for food deliveries and internet shopping. My initial manic spring-cleaning ground to a halt but the daily walks continue to be the highlight of each day. We did manage a week self-catering with the family in the summer when it was wonderful to forget the worries and relax and have fun with the grandchildren. I felt euphoric at getting my vaccination and look forward to some return of normality. Have spoken with **Claire Marshall** and **Julia Tingle.**

Anita Dudley (Armstrong) I feel grateful that I was able to spend a month in Istanbul in January 2020, arriving back in Spain on 3rd February, worried that I had the virus as my cough was horrendous. However, it seems it was just the flu as I kept on tasting food and sniffing odours. How beautiful to see where the Black Sea and the Bosphorous join. Also, the sea of Marmara has wonderful islands, and it is so quaint. New Year 2021 was celebrated in Naples, as usual – another well-kept secret: there are so many fireworks that the whole bay from Naples to Sorrento, containing Pompeii, are filled with smoke and lovely displays.

Mallorca was wonderful. Empty beaches and clean seas, bird song and noticeably less air and noise pollution, but how sad for all the now closed businesses. I feel very lucky to be locked down here, with picnic sites galore, but has been so chilly this month, even with glorious sunshine.

Helen Faircliff (Wienholt) I have been in regular contact, either on Zoom, WhatsApp or emails, with **Sue Barter (Burns)**, **Suz Burroughs (Bradbury)**, **June Cohen (Kefford)**, **Sue Coveney (Hyman)**, **Anne Grocock**, **Lin Lingwood (Maiden)**, **Mandy Lyne (Smith)**, **Claire Marshall** and **Julia Tingle**, which has been great. Somehow friendships formed so many years ago have now made a tremendous difference.

I had the misfortune to break my ankle just as I was preparing to have a week away in my caravan in September. So that idea was scuppered, and I spent the next few months hobbling around.

My granddaughter will be two in April. How time flies. She is tearing around and very chatty and enjoying Nursery. We have WhatsApp'd each day, and played with toys and read stories online, which has worked really well.

Also online, I have started up French lessons again with a lovely teacher whom I met camping in France. She used to come to the campsite to give lessons. It's certainly making the little grey cells work overtime, with subjects ranging from family to ecological matters.

Sandra Russell (Morris) We are so lucky to be in the country with no commuting, stuffy offices etc. We have only heard of one person who has had Covid and they live on the west coast.

Life seems to go on as normal, bridge and lectures online and walks with friend continue - though within guidelines. We have miles of beach as well as farmland and quiet country roads around.

I see pictures of English parks where there are crowds all enjoying sunshine, but no space. As ever, we have rule breakers here too - illegal student house parties, funerals, and foreign travellers. I wonder if they will ever learn any lessons! Son and family in NZ have been back to normal since June! Businesses there have not been affected greatly. Although a few small shops have closed in Cambridge, others have taken their place. That is probably what would have happened anyway.

We were due to get our jabs this week, but snowed in since yesterday, so new appointments made for next week. As we don't see anyone, it doesn't really matter when we get them. We can't travel, so can't meet family or friends. The Christmas presents for my sister and family are still in the spare room. I wonder how a chocolate Santa will go down at Easter! We were to meet halfway and exchange gifts when lockdown occurred.

My sister and I did manage a week away on the west coast in September. It had been booked a year before and we were to be revisiting old haunts. Our family used to spend the month of August there with our grandmother and have great memories. I actually went to primary school there for a year when my father had gone back to St Andrews to do another degree. We had a fabulous time. We took a lovely, reconditioned boathouse right on the edge of a loch. We had seals and herons to watch each evening. The weather was great, and we were able to eat outside every day. Stewart is still waiting to hear when he will get his new hip. I just call him an aged hippy! Should have been last year, but who knows when now.

One good thing to come out of this: I have managed to put spare time to good use and finished the bookshelf of books I have been meaning to read in retirement, 10 years ago! Summer weather was fab, and I made good use of being in the garden every day.

Otherwise puzzles in dark evenings while watching some Netflix. Too much baking being done, figure being undone.

Jane Simpson (Witt) I am very grateful to have a dog and therefore a legitimate excuse to get out every day for a walk during all these restrictions. I loved the summer months, being able to garden 24/7 with a clear conscience that we shouldn't be entertaining or going here and there. Our youngest grandson, who will turn one at the beginning of March, has only known lockdown life with parents around all the time to be at his every beck and call!

However poor John has been, and is still, waiting for a knee replacement and in a lot of pain, but at least we are still above ground and very grateful for it and delighted to have been vaccinated. Those chores that have been put off and put off are gradually getting done, so there are a few pluses! We did manage our postponed trip to Tresco in the Scilly Isles with all the family (15 of us) at the end of September to celebrate John's 80th birthday, which was wonderful, and we enjoyed a two night break at Rick Stein's place in Padstow in December. Our daughter, husband and three little ones escaped London for two weeks over Christmas, so we were very lucky.

Section 32 (1962)

Section Representative:
Sarah Rundle (Milner)

Denise Bittolo (Porter) How difficult it is having family overseas during Covid. My son, in Tenerife, has his own business which unfortunately has been closed for nearly a year, so we have been helping out. Who knows when we will be allowed to go over and see the family? Another son here in Italy with his own business also closed for six months. Thank goodness for Mum and Dad and our pensions! My daughter, a chef/cook is back home with us as restaurants have been closed for months. We are praying vaccinations are going to take care of everything for us. Let us hope so!

Brexit has changed my life too. Barclays were the first to write and tell me I had to close my account with them. We have become aliens if we don't live in the UK. Then a parcel of books arrived the other day and I had company €23 customs charges! I have three more parcels blocked in customs and who knows if I will ever receive them. No more goodies from the UK.

Elizabeth Bryant So much for all of last year's plans. But I did have far more WhatsApps with the friends I would have been holidaying with in Denmark, Australia, and Brunei, as well as a regular cocktail hour with three friends on Sunday evenings.

The first weeks of lockdown were not too bad, with lots of gardening to do and decent weather. But after a while I realised I did not really enjoy books I had carefully kept over the years - who wants to read Antonia White while isolating?

After several weeks, the days became like a string of Sundays in the 50s and I was very relieved when we were allowed out for walks again. It was very good to see **Phil Shaw (Northcroft)** and her husband on a couple of occasions in the summer when they were in the area. I had a great few days with **Mary Hudson** in Lymington, and rented a flat in Weymouth with another friend in October. It was really great to have face-to-face conversations and just to be with other people, doing nothing much. What will the new normal be like?

Mary Hudson - Mary kindly replied to my request but says that she has no news.

Jyotipakshini/Erica Rigg (Harding) - A strange but interesting year living with various levels of lockdown in Glasgow. We have been very fortunate that so far no-one among our family or friends has been struck down seriously by Covid, and my heart goes out to people for whom this has been a hell of a time. Hopefully, the vaccine will ease life for all gradually. As 'The Aged' we have had groceries, newspapers, prescriptions etc. delivered and so have been able to experience a generally peaceful reflective time.

Until this year Michael and I have each enjoyed many groups and activities and were out and about a lot. Now we are together in the house 24 hours a day we decided to take our allowed daily walk separately and I have really appreciated this. I've explored so many nooks and crannies, interesting buildings, quiet green spaces, canal towpaths and rivers in a roughly five-mile radius from the house. Places that I had forgotten or never knew about in the 43 years we've lived here. Fascinating!

Also, with coffee shops and restaurants and even the gym closed, I've taken off weight with all the walking and certainly feel fit. We are lucky that one of our daughters and three of our teenage grandchildren live very near and so we often see them when they pass by on their daily exercise. The wonderful Zoom has made contacting friends and family further away quite accessible, and I've been able to keep up with Buddhist activities without difficulty. Of course, it's different not being with people face to face, but the benefits have been more regular contact with friends in Australia and India. I know I'll be very happy to touch and hug friends and family again one day and I know I'm very fortunate to have someone in the house to hug or be hugged by, but I have learnt a lot about living a quiet unhurried life in my seventy seventh year. I wonder what next year will bring?

Jessamy Reynolds (Smith) - We are lucky to live in the countryside, with lots of fresh air and a garden in which to spend the lockdowns of the past year. Last summer was spent doing lots of gardening, but in the autumn unfortunately my health necessitated life-saving surgery from which I am now recovering, very happy to be alive and still here and being wonderfully looked after by my husband. Convalescing during a lockdown is rather convenient, as we can't go anywhere or see anyone!

We now have most of our family living in Suffolk, so look forward to reconnecting with them once lockdown is lifted. We are still waiting to meet a granddaughter who lives in Geneva and is about to be two years old, but meanwhile she is getting good at FaceTime.

Having missed out on our usual summer opera-going in 2019, we have booked tickets for this year for Glyndebourne, Garsington and Grange Park, in hope. One lovely meeting last year was in September, with **Bridget Nightingale (Wilson)**, who was holidaying in Thorpeness. It was so special to see her again and enjoy some time together. It is more than 60 years since we first met at Westonbirt, in Gloucester House.

Sarah Rundle (Milner) *Cornwall* I found the first lock down so much easier than the second one. I think a great many of us felt like that. Lockdown and Brexit – not sure which is worse. I feel so far away from our daughter and family in France now. Having said that, I haven't seen our son and family for over a year, they live near Oxford. Claire and her boys are nearer (Somerset) and I have seen them.

I did manage to get to Perthshire in September, which was a real bonus. Some of Robin's ashes are scattered up there where we had so many happy times. Loch Rannoch, Rannoch Moor, Rivers Tay and Tilt being the favourites. I am hoping to make it again this year but who knows?

I have managed to continue singing in a virtual choir. Singing into a mobile phone was unimaginable in solo singing lessons with Miss Law all those years ago. I know I say it each year, but how I thank Westonbirt for my great love of singing and classical music. I loved the 12 Doors of Christmas from pupils at Westonbirt.

Sadly, my annual visit to Westonbirt Arboretum in the autumn didn't happen. I am still working in the spring at Caerhays Castle Gardens and, as I write, the huge magnolias are coming out in all their glory. I walk round those gardens with my dogs in the evenings – magical, especially with the sea in the distance.

My sister, **Jane Hopkinson (Milner)**, died last summer. We were not at Westonbirt together as she was older than me, but I have been in touch with some of her friends. She died from motor neurone disease which was misdiagnosed to begin with. A quite dreadful disease and, thankfully, she didn't suffer for too long.

Deborah Soper - In many ways living in Guernsey has made this unusual year a lot easier for me. We went into lockdown March last year but came out at the end of May, in time for a welcome birthday glass of champagne with my friend and my two sons. In a roundabout way, this sparked off a project for Eileen and me, namely exploring the green lanes and starting to prepare a book about sanctuary paths, the green lanes and sanctuary on the island - it seemed so appropriate, as we spent a pretty normal summer safe over here.

For two septuagenarians we did some quite adventurous walks, usually together, accompanied by Fennel, her border terrier. Apart from exercise in general, it helped my new hip bed in, and I even survived tripping on a cliff path. My knee did pour with blood and I was as far away from the car as I could be, but eventually it was glued together in the Princess Elizabeth Hospital!

Eileen has been researching sanctuary paths in the Priaulx Library and I have been attempting illustrations. Things slowed down over Christmas, then the Priaulx shut for a certain amount of reorganisation, then everything shut for the second lockdown! So latterly progress has pretty well stopped. However, next Monday (March 8th) we move into stage two of Guernsey's unlockdown, so we can perhaps get cracking again.

I have not been off the island for at least eighteen months so haven't seen my granddaughter in Shropshire in all that time.

But I am so lucky to be here where walking and swimming are easy (not that I am a winter swimmer, but lots of people are, their numbers seem to be growing all the time) and also lucky both my sons are here. My other three grandchildren are all at university: one finishing medicine next month, another finishing philosophy and politics in the summer and the third about halfway through modern languages at Magdalen College, Oxford.

I have a small garden in which things grow like fury - lots of starry little daffodils out now. I paint and draw a lot, have recently started Pilates (lately on Zoom), and when it is running still go to my post cancer exercise class (that was several years ago now but we all keep going to the class!) The next big event when lockdown allows will be the invasion of builders to sort out the dry rot which has unfortunately appeared. I hope the weather will be good and I can get out of the house!

(Deb sent me two pictures of hers. One of a green lane and one of her garden. I remember being so envious of her talent at Westonbirt SR).

Section 31 (1961)

Section Representative:
Priscilla Llewelyn (Rickard)

First, may I say a big thank you to everyone who has given me news this year - I think we have a record number of contributors. Thank you too to those who have said that they really enjoy reading it! We certainly are a very varied bunch of people (girls) who all emerged from WB in the early 60s. Indeed, we are quite historic now - awful thought, isn't it? So here goes:

Sarah Bays (Fisher) *Gloucestershire* What a weird and trying year. John and I went to the Cheltenham Festival in March and both caught Covid – luckily neither of us was very ill. We are now both vaccinated and forever grateful to our wonderful NHS for getting this organised so efficiently and quickly.

We were blessed with the safe arrival of a fifth grandson in June, so we now have five boys and one granddaughter. It's been the worst part of the pandemic, not to have seen much of the grandchildren, especially baby George.

I think Boris is announcing today that schools are going back on 8th March, and please, for Westonbirt and for all school children, let this have been the last lockdown.

Ellie Bell (Walker) *South Australia* Having lived in South Australia for many years I feel I must pass on my feelings about Covid. Although we were of course struck down over here it has been dreadful to see what you have been going through over the last in the UK. We were so lucky in SA and at the moment have zero active cases. We still have limitations with the number of people at various gatherings and with social distancing, but in general we are back to leading normal lives.

I have been in touch with **Jane Marshall's (Plant)** sons and while having to go through the pains of advanced MS Janie was also struck down by Covid. No-one should have to cope with that.

I was over in the UK and Europe in October 2019. Who was to know then what lay ahead? Maybe you should all move out to beautiful, sunny Adelaide.

Liza Coates (Furse-Roberts) *Edinburgh* Thank you, Priscilla, for keeping us up to the mark! I have been throwing bird seed up on top of the garage. We had a surplus and I decided the biggest bird table was the flat roof, but the problem was how do I get it up there, now that I'm not safe on ladders! Well, the old lacrosse skills came in handy, I found a child's beach spade was just the thing for casting the bird seed aloft. I am also learning Welsh from Duolingo in the hope of having a holiday in Wales this year.

Vanessa Cook (Hall) *North Yorkshire* Still alive I think is important! Running organic Stillingfleet Lodge Garden and plant nursery for 40 years now, six miles from York with a great café, keeps me busy and fit as well as nine grandchildren and two great grandchildren.

Jane Drew (Mason) *Bristol* In happier times I have driven past the school quite frequently on my way to meet a friend in Bibury. I have also occasionally had lunch at the Hare and Hounds.

Lockdown since Christmas has been spent doing a painting-by-numbers picture which took hour after hour! Also, a 'diamond' painting (tiny little beads pressed onto a guide picture). That took hours too -though a few less than the other.

I did quite a few other paintings last year, (not by numbers) and happily tended the garden all summer. I have, however, missed being able to see my two-year-old granddaughter, Anna, who lives in London, though am blessed to have seen my other granddaughter Hannah, aged four (yes, confusion of names!) as she lives just round the corner.

Otherwise, health is mixed. I had to wait six months to have a broken tooth filled, and in addition took four lots of antibiotics to cure a chronic cough (NOT Covid) which I had all year. I used to see people wince if I coughed when out walking, which added to the stress.

Hopefully, better days ahead for all of us since we've been jabbed.

Wendy Earl (Lloyd-Kirk) *Cornwall* I'm in touch with **Jane Kopsch (Capleton), Jane Pilgrim (Begg)** and **Patmalar Thurasingham** who lives in Melbourne.

Life in Cornwall is very good compared to so many places. Being over 70 I am given PTO (permission to officiate) as a Reader (Lay Minister) by our Bishop so am still active in a local parish – all of which has changed dramatically in the past year.

Thank God for the internet and being able to keep in touch via Zoom etc. I also head up five local community groups, all of which aim for the bettering of our town, so I work closely with the local council. This inevitably keeps me very busy. The latest one is CASA (Climate Action St Austell) which springs from being a Novice Tertiary Franciscan and their strong emphasis on caring for our God-given wonderful world. The aim is to encourage everyone to start making all the little changes that are becoming increasingly necessary to reduce our CO^2 emissions.

Weren't we blessed to be educated in such a stunning environment!

Rosie Edgington (Heygate) *Norfolk* Extraordinary times. Nothing of interest in my life. Lots of walking with the dog, occasional trickster bridge, a few Words with Friends, Scrabble, books and television! But we have refurbished The Shed and it is now available for rent by a couple with or without a dog. Beautiful views of Blakeney Point.

I don't like being elderly so many aches and pains but at least we're still alive.

Sue Garden (Button) *London* I don't have any news this year – still going into Parliament every working day. One of the few as most loom down on us on Zoom. Have discovered online bridge and online quizzes which breaks up the solitary days.

Stephanie Grant (James) Brecon Stephanie has spent most of the last year like the rest of us - doing nothing very adventurous. However, she's enjoyed working in their garden last summer when the weather was so good.

They have met up with friends in their bubble, but are frustrated by the problems arising from being so near to the English border. Virtually every rule is different in each country and this makes life very confusing at times, and also very difficult for letting out their lovely longhouse at Nantcol in North Wales.

Stephanie and I meet at the Brecon Arts Society (formerly NADFAS) on Zoom - this has been a great success. But unfortunately, the society is closing as no younger members have come forward to join the committee and continue running the show.

Pennant Huskinson (Iremonger) *Wiltshire* Pennant and I have had a recent catch up, and here is her news.

Penk has now retired. She writes that she suddenly got tired and jaded spending her days in the Criminal Courts and found it incompatible with family life.

Her husband Nicholas also had to retire as a Crown Court Judge when he hit 70, so they sold their house in London and repaired to their house in Malmesbury, which they love. They don't miss London at all, but still go up to the Smoke for fun and to stay at the Garrick.

Penk is having a huge Hartley Botanic greenhouse built behind the Secret Garden. Nicholas plays online/zoom bridge seven days a week.

They have a nine-month-old chocolate tabby point Birman kitten, and are hoping to have one of his uncles from the same pedigree blood line in April.

Like so many others they find it hard not seeing their family, Tom, Vish and their gorgeous four-year-old granddaughter, and they long for better things very soon.

Priscilla Llewelyn (Rickard) ***Monmouthshire*** My news is as follows: I'm now living in a house near Abergavenny that I renovated just before lockdown and it is proving a great success, with plenty to keep me occupied, as required.

I also play bridge online and I'm very happy to make up a four, anywhere in the world, if needed!

I have been writing my autobiography - sounds a bit odd, but in fact I set up a business rather against the odds at the end of the 1980s, and I thought it might be quite interesting for future generations to read about it. This rather fanciful thought is based on my own wish that I had had something similar from my grandparents.

The book is at the publishers as I write this, so I am waiting with bated breath to see what the family's reaction will be when it appears. Somebody suggested that I ask friends from long ago to write out their memories and it has been absolutely amazing what has been forthcoming, Including some boyfriends of yesteryear whose copy has actually had to be heavily edited to get past the censors! If anyone else feels inspired I would be happy to give some further tips that I have learnt along the way, if they're useful.

All best wishes to everyone for a rapidly improving year. *(Ed Please ask your Section Rep for Priscilla's contact details).*

Jane Merritt (Wilkinson) *North Carolina, USA* Due to Covid, my year has been drastically changed. No prison ministry, no in-church services on Sundays, and no choir and no gym. My pastoral visits were cut out, so I have actually enjoyed a quieter life taking daily walks with my husband in the neighbourhood and participating in Zoom meetings at church. Our dog loves having us at home. We have started clearing out our home and getting rid of stuff we no longer need - it seems an endless job!

I cannot run any more due to some medical issues, so this quieter life has allowed me to continue with physical therapy at home to improve my balance.

Let us hope that things will get back to normal soon. I miss seeing my son and family in Denmark and I will visit as soon as travel restrictions are lifted.

Jane Mounsey (Bennion; Irwin) Wiltshire Who has any news these days?! I haven't any except I'm happy in my garden and am so grateful I have one and don't live in a high rise. In fact, my garden (created by my wonderful husband who died in 2018) is open on June 20th from 2 pm for The Garden Scheme and on June 21st for Youth Action Wiltshire from 6pm - canapés and booze - what a GREAT party that will be!

Susan Nock (Constance) ***Gloucestershire*** It has been an extraordinary year. I was lucky that my children, grandchildren and two sons-in-law decided early in March that there would be a lockdown and requested board and lodging with us on the farm for a few weeks in the spring and that then extended into the summer. We started with twelve and finished with thirteen when Rosie had another baby in May! It was a massive shopping and feeding operation, but my two sons-in-law are excellent and very competitive cooks and made life easy.

Now that Gerard and I have had too many birthdays we thought it was time to buy a smaller house and retire to a nearby village. We bought a pretty old farmhouse and set about refurbishing it and made a plan to move in the new year. I sent out change of address cards and started clearing out 40 years of stuff. Then we had a change of heart and decided we would miss our way of life and would stay on the farm for a few more years. Now I have to empty the packing cases, send out another batch of address cards cancelling the original ones and wait for the charity shops to re-open!

I have lost some good friends in the past year, a few from Covid, which makes me want to keep in touch, and I really enjoy the yearbook.

Meg Paige (Fleury) ***Bath*** This year has been one of ups and downs:

A down. For us from March last year we were locked in like others and missed a trip to Canada.

An up. Our daughter-in-law did our shopping and we enjoyed the wonderful summer in the garden. It gave us time to paint and plant vegetables that thrived.

A down. Our son was diagnosed with cancer in the summer and we were devastated.

An up. He had a huge op and a course of chemo and is now in remission.

Another down. One of his sons caught Covid hand had to isolate for Richard's sake.

An up. He only had a mild attack and recovered quickly.

A down. It started my hair turning grey!

Two ups. We became great-grandparents in June and September to a great-granddaughter and a great-grandson. Our eldest two grandsons had increased our family. Another great-granddaughter is due this summer.

A down. We don't see enough of these new arrivals due to the restrictions.

An up. We have visited them both once in the lockdown break and had cuddles.

Another up. Our miniature wirehaired dachshund had five puppies. They are now four months and gone to loving families who send me texts and videos on their development.

Another up: We have kept one who is a joy and a great addition to our other two dogs all who have kept us sane this year.

So, on balance the ups outweigh the downs.

Hope this is of some use. *(Yes, it's great, thanks. PL)*

Sue Patchett (Greenwood) *Sydney, NSW (Fascinating, but horrific news, all featured on our screens this March - PL)* We are having what the media call a rain-bomb at the moment. Talk about flooding rains! A couple's house washed down the river, the worst thing being it took their Jack Russell with it. Being a dog-lover, that finished me off!! The main dam for Sydney is overflowing and they have to let more water out - about the same amount as Sydney Harbour every day. Hard to grasp really, but it means major evacuations if it continues.

Otherwise, we have been lucky with Covid and have been locked down but not nearly as badly as some countries.

Charlotte my 16-year-old grandchild, cut off her long hair for the Ponytail Project for cancer. Her school collected $40,000. I thought that was quite impressive!

That's my offering for this year. Stay well everyone.

Angela Sellings (Marson) *Berkshire* Another year on and again they have had to cancel the 90th birthday celebrations. Let's hope we can have a get together next year. We're waiting to see if we can get away this summer. I have done a lot of walking over the last months on my own and occasionally with a friend, but it will be lovely when we can meet friends in a group again.

I read the report about the repair to the lake at Westonbirt with interest. I well remember it when we were there and I think I can remember skating on it one winter, or is my mind playing tricks? It is 60 years ago!

Hendrina Willoughby-Ellis (Moerman) *Lincolnshire* Henny and I have recently had a catch up and she told me she had no news. However, I think otherwise!

She has three children, a son in London, and a son and daughter, one in New Zealand and one in Australia. Needless to say, she misses them and is hoping to visit them in 2022.

Following gaining her science degree, Henny worked as the science editor of the *Schools Science Review* for many years. Now she is retired and misses the work. However, ten years ago she and her husband bought a medieval building in Kings Lynn and have had a fascinating time restoring it and absorbing its history in the process.

One of Henny's daughters is an archaeologist, and she has had fascinating visits to Albania, Bermuda and Syria to visit her at work on the archaeological sites.

Like everyone else, Henny can't wait for this Lockdown to be lifted and for life to get back to normal again.

Gillian Wynes (Ross Goobey) *Somerset* After not being allowed in the restaurant during lockdown and having our lunch in our apartments, we are still not allowed in the restaurant, but hoping to be allowed back in soon. In March last year I went to a live performance of *Shrek* locally. I had seen it at The Hippodrome in Bristol with my granddaughter and thought the local showing was better. A week later we were in the first lockdown. A friend and I went out to dinner at a local hotel when we were allowed. That is all I've done this year.

Thanks again everyone. As you would expect, I have everyone's contact details, so if anyone would like to be put in touch I'd be happy to help. I'll need to ask the other person first if it is ok, due to the current rules in the UK. Priscilla

Section 30 (1960)

Section Representative:
Jane Reid (Bottomley)

2020 was 60 years after the last of Section 30 and their contemporaries left Westonbirt. The plan had been to mark the anniversary by meeting at the AGM and enjoying the associated events at Westonbirt. Instead, a set of Zoom meetings were held that day, starting at 08:00, 15:00 and 22:00 BST to enable members around the globe to join. Information of known attendance plans was circulated shortly before – which meant that many increased the number of meetings they would attend, and some managed all three! **Jeannie Astill (Mackenzie), Ann Beard (Harverson), Bodhiniya (Ann Udal), Pepi Cowell (Bowring), Pat Davidson (Weaver), Phoebe Field (Northcroft), Leggie Godwin (Neill), Jenny Greenwood (Bawtree), Janet Kingston (Oakeley), Joan Madonko (Scott), Carol Mullin (Rostron), Jane Palestini (Macfadyen), Juliet Peel (de Galleani), Jane Reid (Bottomley), Anne Rennie (McCullagh), Rosemary Somers (Fuchs-Marx),** and **Sallie Sullivan (Sanderson)** attended. **Elizabeth Hawken (Avens), Avril Goldstein (Le Tissier)** and **Roma Part (Thorpe)** were unable to Zoom and sent friendly messages.

Rosemary Cartwright (Herald) (not an Association member) acknowledged mailings.

Phoebe Field (Northcroft), in New Zealand, did not mind the lockdown but sympathised with others with the bug on their doorstep. The family tree had kept her busy for many years, and she had learnt a good deal about the past times.

Elizabeth Hawken (Avens) resumed use of email.

Janet Kingston (Oakeley) had trouble starting the car (scarcely used in the year since the first lockdown) when she needed to fill up with petrol! It had struck her that she must be the only WB girl still using her school laundry bag as well as PE and hair ones. Her mother obviously made them well. Janet and her family were well; she was very glad that they had made the early visit to Australia last year.

Their daughter was managing quite well, even if they did have about three WhatsApp calls a day! Both daughters had had to work right through, and, because his father was also a key worker, their grandson hadn't missed any school. Being in Tier 2 over Christmas meant the UK folk could meet up for lunch, even if they did sit at separate tables in the lounge with windows and patio doors open wide!

Janet had not done anything news-shattering in the year except try to keep fit. She hoped others were well.

Jane Reid (Bottomley) was amused to find that the pandemic meant that Sainsburys became their food-supplier, providing the Nectar points which paid for most of the cost of the simple printer that was needed because access to her husband's college printer was unavailable because of the pandemic!

Doing a hieroglyphs course over Zoom was almost better than Real Life because of undisputed use of the table space, which was large enough to include a 32-inch television as an extra-large monitor for the laptop (used for the course) while leaving room for the printer, as well as two desktop PCs and a tablet that displayed all the crib files she could find on the web (she needs all the help she can get for such courses!) – and still leave room for the necessary papers to write on.

In the summer between lockdowns, one of Jane's nieces met the parents of her newish boyfriend and was startled, first to find that his mother had been to Westonbirt (**Anne Much**, contemporary with Section 28 or so) and remembered Jane. Then it turned out that his father had known Jane at university and had been claimed as a distant relative. (Even that had a slight WB connection: **Elizabeth Reisz** had wanted to give a gender-balanced birthday party too soon after the start of their first term for her to have widened her acquaintance sufficiently; Jane had suggested as a potential guest a sixth cousin whose existence she had only been told of the month before.)

Rosemary Somers (Fuchs-Marx) emailed in February: "What a year it's been! The most important news is that my husband, Tony, and I continue Covid free and vaccinated. We now seem to have been in lockdown for almost a calendar year.

"Last January we enjoyed a trip to Germany, meeting up with other family members from afar. In March we had a smaller family gathering. I note we went for a lovely walk with spring flowers in the woods. In summer we managed to escape to Dorset by the sea for a few days during a heat wave.

"Our street celebrated its newly strengthened sense of community by having a festival on the afternoon of Saturday 5th September with bunting and balloons. There was singing, dancing, cakes, and jewellery-making, as well as a celebration of our multinational community with flags. Residents and friends could walk up and down and visit each other's stalls. In the evening, the communal garden was opened and inside there were children's races, music, poems, songs, personal storytelling, (Tony told his), a performance by our local am-dram group and a closing circle dance!

"The Covid pandemic has also encouraged us all to develop and utilise new online skills. We have all learned to appreciate nature more than before. So, we have really enjoyed our little back garden that Tony lovingly tends. We have explored nearby parks, some of which became more accessible when the traffic was so quiet. I made delicious bread for the first time, but this had to stop, as we put on Corona-kilos!

"The whole family managed to get together at our son Mark's house at the end of August for our 55th wedding anniversary. I do various physical exercises, as well as learn Spanish, in online classes. The teenage grandchildren are receiving online learning. While they miss their friends by not going to school, distractions from lessons are reduced. Helen, Mark, and their spouses are all able to work from home, saving commuting time. Of course, not everyone is so fortunate, and our hearts go out to those who live alone, have lost their jobs or are in financial difficulties.

"We managed to have a late summer holiday for five days in September. We went to visit Tony's brother Michael in Cornwall, breaking the journey in a lovely country hotel in Dartmoor. Tony has been writing his life story and I am illustrating it with photographs. To this end, we went to the farm, Tregantle, where he lived during the war (1944-1947) on the way to Michael's. Amazingly the current owners, who were happy to show us round, remembered Tony's mother's name! The farmhouse was only slightly changed from how Tony remembered it. We came home via Bristol, to visit granddaughter Molly who is at university there, and were also able to see the house where Tony lived before Tregantle farm.

"However, we count our blessings. We have each other and are in pretty good health. Otherwise, life goes boringly on here in London, seeing our friends, children and grandchildren only by Zoom."

Bridget Towle had reluctantly become the President of the Leicester Literary and Philosophical Society; she felt that the lecture programme was well above her intellectual level. The most challenging part was that the lectures were held on Zoom. It was strange speaking without seeing or hearing a reaction; maybe fortunate.

Section 29 (1959)

Section Representative:
Lin Coleman

For obvious reasons this hasn't been a year for much news, but some of us managed to get a Zoom group together in February. Despite lockdown we've all been pretty active.

Joan (Nonie) Beckingsale (Hills) We belong to a community group which used to go into the local school regularly to act out Bible stories. When that came to a juddering halt, we started making videos to distribute to several schools in the area. At one stage, we dressed up as various characters and were filmed individually in front of a green screen; with further lockdowns, we just record our voices. It was all a bit alarming at first, but we are getting used to it. Hope we can get back to singing sometime - if we can remember how to.

Sue Bowden (Humpidge) is about to start lambing, taking turns with her husband on the night shifts. They also have a donkey, and two Shetland ponies. She has eight smashing grandchildren and is currently writing her memoirs, with lots of happy memories recorded in her Westonbirt diaries.

Helen Brown (Todd) lives in north Cumbria and is a botanical recorder in the county.

Lin Coleman (Hutton) is still working part-time as a psychotherapist in London (on Zoom), gardening and singing in a vocal jazz choir, Take Twenty, (on Zoom again!)

Libby Houston I'm still scrambling up and down the Avon Gorge checking on the rare plants and trees. I've just requalified for another three years as a rope access technician, to abseil officially on the cliffs doing practical conservation work – all quite acceptable during lockdown as very socially distanced! Meanwhile, great to get back to indoor climbing after more than a year's Covid ban (and the pub afterwards!) I'm in touch with **Jennifer Scully (nee Parker)**.

Linda Northcroft (Angell) writes that she is now Linda Angell as she re-married in March 2020 one week before lockdown. They had a church service in the village where she'd previously lived - the last time many of their friends and family were able to be together. She's had one cataract surgery and is waiting for the second eye to be done. The most annoying thing is not being able to drive for the time being as she would like to explore Staffordshire and take her dogs somewhere different for their walks. Hoping for better times.

Myrth Russell (Hudson) is enjoying being up in Scotland, and tells us: "My 14-year-old granddaughter is carrying on the musical tradition and getting excellent results in her clarsach and flute exams. The clarsach is not only lovely to play, but it means she can play for weddings, and earn her way!"

Section 28 (1958)

Section Representative:
Sue Hicks (Harker)

Thanks to all who replied this year. It is lovely to hear from you, all the more because of our lack of normal contact with friends and family.

Sheila Astbury (Stuart) observes that the enforced slower pace of life has helped to camouflage our natural inclination to be less active with increasing age, but it will be exciting to see how life changes and society adapts as we emerge into a new normal routine. She has been fortunate to have frequent contact with grandchildren, family and friends through technology but looks forward to when we have direct contact.

Jennie Bland (May) has been doing something we would all find difficult, and writes: "My life is going through a huge change as I packed up Blissamore and downsized to a flat in London. Making decisions about much of what has been my life for 60 years: Keep? Give? Sell? Charity shop? Free-cycle? Dump? etc. So many choices to make, the most difficult being about the small things which remind me of very happy days, things the children and then the grandchildren made for me, boxes of photographs, letters from friends now gone, including dearest **Judy (Morris)** whom you will all remember. I hate to admit it, but some of these will be sent (temporarily I hope) into a store from which I will take them and sort - when I've less to do. (???)

"I've always lived in the country and in fact the Covid restrictions have meant that I've appreciated all that this life offers even more. I will miss the walks, the horses, the garden and all the people here in a busy community. However, one great comfort is that I've sold the house to a wonderful family with four young children. The house will love them and they it!

"AND London has so much to offer; when at last they reopen I'll relish the theatres, exhibitions, and lectures, and having many friends nearby.

"So... Life moves on. Like most of you, I'm 81 and so I value every day and all those I love hugely. Good times ahead."

Elisabeth Blood (Plant) notes that now, a number of us have reached 80, and are still here! She had just had a knee replacement, very painful but ok now. Surgeon son Henry in Kent had been helping with the jabs and trying to operate. Some of the grandchildren had gone back to universities but not to school. She can't wait to go on holiday, would love some sunshine, but thinks it will be a while yet.

Paula Bradfield (Stovold) Paula was suffering from lockdown apathy and had not been in touch with WB news for a few years. It was lovely to hear from her again. She has Parkinson's, which really slows her down. It took at least three years to get diagnosed, a very difficult time, and that was about four years ago. So, lots of years have really been just managing. She has been in touch with **Wendy Garforth (Evershed).**

Sue Hicks (Harker) The last year has flown by. It's spring again already. The internet has made it possible to adapt, although life is not the same. I am in the local U3A and the monthly talks are excellent, without even having to drive there first. I just need to get a coffee. I run a French conversation group, and more people are attending on Zoom than used to come to the venue. We miss our holidays abroad and look forward to exploring the UK when permitted. We can see one daughter and family who live nearby, but the family in Ireland feels cut off. I wonder what the situation will be next year? Our beloved black cat died, and we now have two rather wild little rescue cats who keep us on our toes. On the plus side, we are enjoying a more peaceful life, and John has become an excellent cook.

Penelope Jepson I have been in touch with Penelope for the first time in many years but she has not sent in any news. *(Ed. Great that you've made contact!)*

Lesley Scoular wonders if *anyone* has any news? She says "However, with spring there's hope. One lesson I've learnt about myself during the past year is that I'm unable to pursue interests such as painting and yoga through classes on Zoom: I need to be physically present with the other class members. Sadly, my lung condition precludes any more hills (no new Munros) but, when circumstances allow, I keep busy with friends and varied activities. Eightieth birthday celebrations have been on hold since last June. My lockdown companion has been four-footed/pawed: a newly-rehomed young cat. He behaves like a wayward teenager."

Margaret Squires (Renshaw) It is very hard to find something good to say about this year. We had developed a routine of local walks when we decided we might like to extend our range and got the bikes out. Alas, Roger managed to hit a bollard, break a hip and arm, and landed up in hospital where even I, down the phone, could diagnose his room-mate as having Covid. He was eventually removed in paroxysms of coughing so awful that they could hardly fail to hear it, and there was a week of phony war when Roger felt fine, until he didn't! Luckily, he pulled through. I have nothing but praise for the police who extracted me from behind a stuck mattress, which was blocking the stairs, and got the bed base down for me. The OT who told me I needed it there said they didn't help, nor did the community group that had sprung up, so I had set about doing it myself.

Roger had given me a Fitbit for Xmas 2020 so I made sure to clock up a healthy number of steps each day, and that and weather watching kept me sane. I send weather photos to the BBC each day, and once in a blue moon they get picked for the forecast.

Sadly, my business partner of 37 years caught Covid in a care home and died. I now phone her widower every week in the same home. He still doesn't know that 17 people died there.

On the bright side, we had our first jag (jag in Scotland, jab in England) a fortnight ago. Grandson WhatsApps us from Belgium and former hillwalking group from Birmingham and Oz.

Catherine Whittingham (Norman Moses) I think that like many, my greatest achievement this past year has been to stay alive. Like so many of us, we have been fortunate in being able to cocoon in comfort with good food delivered very easily.

We moved from our house in May, which was not easy; it was large, and despite our condo being spacious there was a huge amount of stuff to dispose of . Luckily, the young family who bought our house wanted a lot of our furniture and all our garden implements, which helped immensely. I am not sure I love condo life but it is hard to judge in the context of the pandemic. We had planned to lock the door and do all the travelling we had not done while we were raising our granddaughter. Best laid plans!

Probably like everyone I have read a lot, tried to improve my knowledge of history, and I certainly know more about US politics than I want, CNN has been quite a feature in our lives during the past few months.

We Zoom and FaceTime with friends and family and have been able to walk with friends. We played golf in the summer and I am thankful that despite being quite arthritic I can still hit the ball.

My family has been lucky, our son is a clean energy financial consultant who works from home anyway. His wife runs a catering business and has been doing take-out and teaching children how to cook on Zoom. The teenage children have been in school more than out, and, since they live in the Canadian Rockies, lockdown has been fairly pleasant. Our granddaughter now lives on Vancouver Island and has not been too restricted, but is doing her university courses online, although I am not sure how one does biology online.

I think I have been lucky with a circle of friends who have kept me entertained with assorted videos and a lot of Covid humour!

John is well, although unlike a lot of husbands has not taken over the cooking but he vacuums! Canada is behind the UK in terms of vaccination but I hope to receive mine in the next few weeks.

Section 27 (1957)

Section Representative:
Angela Potter (Tracy)

I'm sorry to report that I now have three less correspondents this Spring. Ann Williamson died last summer. She was a great supporter of Westonbirt and frequently attended reunions. Then at Christmas time, both **Rhonnie Watts (Murray)** - remember her? with flaming red hair and a keen lacrosse player - and **Elisabeth Abrahams (Langford)** died. I'm sure most of you remember her too. The Langfords were amongst the very few families who had three daughters at Westonbirt (Dorchester) at the same time.

My personal news is pretty minimal. We have enjoyed our empty diaries and have both completed several neglected projects, although we still have quite a lot left! Apart from fewer foreign holidays, life went on here much as normal until December, but since then our household has been very busy as we are home to three adult grandchildren whose parents live abroad. We've become an offshore university! The amount they eat is astonishing, but I'm glad to say that we only have one left here now.

My guiding of visitors round the school and its gardens has stopped of course, but with virtually no pupils in residence the Holfords of Westonbirt Trust has taken the opportunity to push on with some essential restoration. The newly repaired lake is looking wonderful, but there are many other projects in hand, including the restoration to active service of the only (yes, the very last!) remaining greenhouse behind the courtyard classrooms.

It has been a very strange year for all of us, but whereas this time last year there was a distinct possibility of Armageddon, now we can be enormously grateful to medical science for holding back that possibility, and indeed be pleased to be over 80. Inevitably many anniversaries and holidays were cancelled, and we are all now just that much older to enjoy them, but the general mood is optimism – after all, we survived the war! The news from my correspondents has been fairly cheerful. Several of them have made very good use of the enforced leisure. In response to my various emails over the year I have also heard from **Jane McCarthy (Hellyer)**, **Rachel Palmer (Philips)**, **Sandy Elkington (Johnson)** and **Bridget Maslin (Coleman)**.

Joan Allan (Blakeborough) In early March last year I was in Scotland but managed to get the last flight from Glasgow to Malaga! How fortunate was that! Douglas had managed to fall in my absence and damage his ribs and his left wrist quite badly so he could do little for himself and could not drive.

Our lockdown in Spain was complete - not allowed out of the front door, not even into our communal gardens, and we could only go, singly, to the shops for food and/or the chemist. We are fortunate to have a very large terrace as we joined two flats together, so were able to exercise on that. We actually enjoyed the first lock down! Douglas decided right away to turn out the cupboards, many of which had not been looked at in over 30 years! He also completed his own study, with all his family and other files, and we both embarked on the photos. This was a horrendous task. By mid-May things were more relaxed and we were allowed to play golf. We drove back to Scotland in July.

We did manage to see Hugo and family twice when we were in Scotland in the summer and made a huge detour to visit Nick and family in Kent before catching the ferry back to Spain from Plymouth in September. Colin and family have been locked up in Trinidad for a year now, though they have managed to have quite a few trips across to nearby Tobago as it is all the same country.

Our boys have been absolutely marvellous at keeping in touch with us and all three contact us at least once a week. I sincerely thank God for the internet as we can see all the family. We had a lovely Zoom with all 16 of them on Boxing Day. Since we returned here in September l have been engrossed with a newly found relative in getting the Blakeborough family tree sorted out and filling in the gaps. In the autumn l decided not to return to golf and my arthritis is much less painful. Our second lockdown has not been nearly so extreme, and we have been able to meet with two other people at a time in our home. All cafes and restaurants now are open until 6pm but one can only have six at a table. Curfew for all at 10pm. Once or twice, we have had to scramble to get home in time!

Barbara (aka Tucker) Anderson I am lucky that, at 81, I am very well. Like most people I have been pottering at home, and the best part of most days is the permissible 'exercise' walk! I belong to a U3A Writing for Pleasure group, and, for something to do during the lockdowns, I have put a selection of the pieces that I have written together, and they are at the printers at the moment. This has been quite a steep learning curve as I haven't done anything like this before!

Judith Briggs (Walker) My news is rather sparse, like everyone else's, but at least we didn't succumb to the dreaded virus and while all our plans for last year had to be cancelled, we consider ourselves fortunate in that we have had space around us so could always walk at least around where we live, unlike many others stuck in small apartments or in shacks in townships in this country *(South Africa)*.

We live in a small complex with just four units but with a long driveway to the road, so our routine was up and down the drive each day to keep moving! At that stage we weren't allowed out to exercise so that had to do. We were able to get to Cape Town last September and again in December so were able to catch up with son Guy and family who live there.

We are sad not to have seen the American family for over two years now, as last year should have been a great get-together – instead, we have learnt to use Zoom and YouTube to tune into events and Whatsapp for more phone calls to keep connected. Alexandra's daughter Claire is now at the University of Maryland and enjoying it, though all the classes are online, of course. But the important thing is that they are all well. Alexandra is a doctor in a paediatric practice so has been going to work throughout (stressful though), while the rest of the family have studied (Max and Charlie, 17, in their penultimate high school year) or worked from home (son-in-law Craig, a prosecutor with the District Attorney's office in Boston). The Cape Town family have also learned to work/study online, and although not easy, are getting through it.

We still await vaccination roll-out plans, as so far here there is only enough to start protecting the frontline health workers. But us oldies will be next in line and look forward to that protection. Like so many others I read a lot during lockdown last year and cleaned and cooked - especially making lots of marmalade!

South Africa started out well with handling the virus, but has not been able to continue in the same vein. Corruption is still rife and while it is being exposed, people are still getting away with it. There have been a lot of illogical rules imposed - meant well, I suppose, but tiresome, and broken by many. Banning tobacco gave a huge impetus to the illicit tobacco trade, and banning the sale of alcohol added to the frustration felt by all, even though it did decrease the hospital trauma admissions! But we keep going, and most activities can continue via Zoom or similar - one just misses the greater human contact.

Christabel Cumberlege (Jacques) Big news for Mike and me in that last September we downsized. Downstairs it is smaller, but upstairs there is a huge room for children and grandchildren to stay, when allowed. So, we have been busy during lockdown, with ideas for small alterations which we will get our friendly local workmen and women to put in place when allowed. It was immaculate when we moved in, quite daunting. It has now acquired the familiar Cumberlege clutter. We are still at Norton-sub-Hamdon, and now have a delightful small garden and will plant climbing French beans up the trellising.

Vanessa Evans (Llewellyn) My news briefly is: Vaccinations now done, no side effects. I have been able to continue my two half-days a week work. Still enjoy teaching my four recorder music students. The singing and country dance has been cancelled since last year unfortunately. Husband son and daughter are well. I recently broke my wrist so I probably will not be able to do my weekly swim at the YMCA pool for two months.

Jennifer Grant-Rennick (Lang) Very sorry to hear of the death of **Rhonnie Watts** and **Elisabeth Abrahams**. I do remember them both quite well. It is amazing how much one can remember of one's school days even when large slices of one's past remain a complete blank. I am the author of several books on London's livery companies, as well as a modern romantic novel, of naughty goings on in the hunting field, and I have been occupying myself during the pandemic with writing my life story for the amusement of my friends and family. It is a tale worth telling. I started work in the House of Lords, then became a secretary in the House of Commons, spent a year helping a deb's mum, taking over from **Bridget Frost (Kell)**, and finally three years in the Savoy Hotel press office, before arriving in Cherington, to ride, write and, finally, to marry a publisher of sporting books. *My Lucky Life* is the life, loves and affairs of an old Westonbirt girl born and bred in Scotland but educated down south. It is available for £10 from **friends@tetburyhospital.co.uk** and all proceeds will go to: The Friends of Tetbury Hospital, Malmesbury Road, Tetbury GL8 8XB. *(This has been highly recommended by **Rachel Palmer (Philips)**, and I certainly plan to buy a copy myself! AP)*

Rowena Ginns (Cullin) We are safe and well but haven't had any physical contact with James in Hong Kong, Jonathan in the New Forest (working from home at present), or the three grandsons in London, whom we hope to catch up with, maybe at the end of April, when we can go back to our flat. In the meantime, we have made good use of the time, initially in the good weather last summer to work in the garden and de clutter outside storage, and over this last lockdown, a massive amount of decluttering inside. We are hoping that by the end of June, we may get some coaching activities again. I do speak to **Sheila Astbury** and **Sue Hicks (Harker)** from time to time and correspond with **Vanessa Evans (Llewellyn)**.

Alison Reed (Hill) I am fortunate to have a good network of local friends, and being able to walk in nearby Regent's Park has been really helpful. I have enjoyed observing the different seasons, and now with the spring flowers and blossom appearing, it is particularly cheering. I have started to play a bit of online bridge, and manage to Zoom in on occasional lectures and meetings, but I greatly regret that my computer skills are so limited. The news of **Rhonnie's** death was a real shock and sadness, as she has been such a good friend ever since our days at Westonbirt. I was especially pleased to be able to watch her funeral service. I look forward to being able to get to Northumberland again, and possibly a holiday in Scotland later in the year. More immediately it will be a relief to get the second vaccination. I am contented living in London and, although I probably should have moved, having a stairlift installed when Anthony was ill, and which I am keeping, does make it more possible to stay here.

Section 26 (1956)

Section Representative:
Angela Potter (Tracy)

Felicity Coulthard (Scott) I'm still here, living in the same house (since 1966) with my family next door caring for me. I'm more arthritic, and as movement is painful I spend far too much time reading, doing puzzles, and watching TV. I still enjoy eating and drinking. Lockdown is not a problem. In fact, I'm not sure I want it to end! We are lucky to have telephone and email, though I have managed to avoid Facebook etc. I do Zoom, but without the camera. I am perfectly content.

Jane Hancock (Quayle) Needless to say we have done no travelling this year. We had to cancel three cruises and eventually got the money refunded. The main event of the year was our diamond wedding anniversary in August. We were able to have a small family lunchtime celebration in our daughter's garden. We were fortunate in that it rained all morning while they were getting everything ready, but the sun came out at noon and we had a lovely afternoon. The other important thing on the horizon is that our eldest granddaughter is expecting a baby in April so hopefully we will be joining the great-grandparents' club. We have fortunately escaped the virus so far. We are well supported by neighbours in the village. We should get our second vaccination in three weeks time.

Valerie Mitchell (Noad) NO news, really! We're still fine, thankfully - awaiting our second jabs, and longing to see our children and the grandchildren. Thanks to letters kept by family, we are writing up our memoirs: our childhoods abroad, boarding schools there and here (and early working lives abroad), all SO different from our kids' and grandchildren's lives - the latter have been home-educated for the past four years. I am AMAZED, there are hundreds, if not thousands of mums doing this!

Rachel Palmer (Philips) re: **Margaret Jackson (Grubb)** Just had a good chat with Margaret. She is her usual cheerful self and busy but missing her large adult family all down south. She and Bob had a diamond wedding last year. Saw her a couple of years ago in London.

Cyrilla Potter (Monk) I am hoping 2021 may be happier, as all exciting plans were squashed by Covid! It was the first time I have ever spent Christmas alone, also my birthday and all the other festive days. Good to keep in touch with my daughters and grandchildren on video. However, one missed the warmth of human contact. I have had my first part of the AstraZeneca vaccine and I am tremendously impressed by the marvellous organisation and kind, helpful volunteers at the centre. I had a reaction after the jab and was kept back for three quarters of an hour - very re-assuring.

Anne Renard (Matthews) I'm just very grateful for all my books, which I've been sorting and enjoying. Quite a few, which I still have, were 21st presents when I was reading Classics at Cambridge. One of my treasures is a tiny volume of *The Iliad*, found for me by Miss Snow, who many of us from the 50s may remember. Best wishes to everyone for a more settled year I hope you find lots of good reads in 2021!

Oriel Rogers-Coltman (Corbett) I have some sad news myself. Wyndham died in September. He hadn't been 100% for a couple of months and was diagnosed with bowel cancer which had spread to the liver at end of July. It was too late for treatment by then but, in a way, it was a relief because chemo is not pleasant. It was sad that we could only have such a small funeral, but for all that we did him proud, and he is buried in the churchyard about 200 yards from here. We were married 60 years ago in April 1960. The wretched first lockdown meant we had to cancel the celebration party we were going to have in May. It was so lucky that we moved south in 2014. All our children are very close and are being a huge support. I have no intention of moving house, even though it could have been considered too big for two of us. It's easy to live in, in the middle of a nice village which is at the bottom of Lucinda's drive. I hope I will manage alright - I don't mind being on my own really and thank goodness the garden is much smaller than in Northumberland. Also, Simon (younger son) persuaded us to get a robot mower last summer which is a great little helper! Our grandchildren don't stay here as much these days. They are all quite grown up - two gainfully employed, seven at university and just one still at school.

Valerie Sill (Marsland) Lockdown hasn't bothered me too much as I have plenty to occupy me on the land and in the house. I have, of course, missed my social life, not that I have a packed diary these days but, in normal times I enjoy meeting friends for meals out, mainly at lunch time. I now look forward to April 12th when we can go to our holiday homes BUT not before I have been to the hairdressers on the 13th! I never imagined that in my dotage I would have my hair on my shoulders! I had my second vaccination last week so will soon feel more relaxed moving around when allowed.

Section 25 (1955)

Section Representative:
Angela Potter (Tracy)

Beth Barrington Haynes My news will be short so as not to depress others. I'm being treated for lung cancer at Chelsea and Westminster Hospital, which mercifully is quite near where I live, alongside the Hurlingham Club, and with a nice Thames-side path for residents. Soon after that diagnosis, it emerged I also had mild lymphoma, and much later a leaking heart valve! So, in the hands (brains?) of Oncology, Haematology and Cardiology, with occasional incarcerations in the hospital for tests, so I am very busy.

I am shielding in my flat with swollen feet so cannot put on any footwear, even trainers! The prognosis is not good, but I benefit from a wonderful bubble-mate and have many friends here – plus long-standing well-wishers which is encouraging. Like us all (?), we have obeyed the lockdown rules. I have a superb shopper friend and two others who get cash from the bank for me. I most certainly am not lonely. District nurses visit twice a week to redress my legs - today an improvement due to diuretic. It is nearly a full-time job just puzzling out the almost-always incorrect hospital appointments! What is lovely is that both **Bridget Frost (Kell)** and her sister **Caroline** are living here, having done up two wonderful seventh-floor flats. Of course, no get-togethers since lockdown but maybe again SOON?

Alyn Denholm (Paisley) Not a lot of news! I have been refining my photography skills, or lack of them, online, also book clubs, bridge, and family on zoom. Have invested in an e-bike which is the best thing ever and can now get around the place, within restrictions, and get my exercise.

All in all, I have been very fortunate living where I do, although I do miss my family. Hopefully, that will sort itself out this summer.

Bridget Frost (Kell) What sad news about **Lizzie, (Elisabeth Abrahams)** - I shared a dormitory with her on and off for six years and learnt to sleep through anything after her wheezing! I shall miss her a lot.

I have had a son with me for two months, but he returns to Canada tomorrow. I am lucky having a daughter near (although she is in hospital as I write - she has lung cancer - but should be out early next week) and another son 10 mins away, AND my sister is in another block near to me. We also have the Hurlingham Club grounds to walk in every day.

Jill Gibson (Connor) I was very sad to learn of **Elisabeth Abraham**'s death. She was such a very brave lady and her service, which I was privileged to follow, was uplifting. I had spoken to her just a couple of weeks before she died, and she was her usual cheerful self. Like everyone else, my news is minimal - we are vaccinated but being careful and doing little outside the house and garden. But with the sun shining, as it is this morning, hopefully the garden will start to benefit soon. Our eldest son, Douglas, is now in Canada with his wife, working as defence and military adviser (what we used to call defence attaché) for three years. All complicated by Covid quarantine regulations, which makes travel difficult, particularly for the family to visit, which would normally be every school/university vacation. But he is enjoying the challenges - all very different from his last posting in Israel. We hope to be able to visit, maybe next spring. Something to look forward to. The rest of the family continue well, homeschooling hopefully coming to an end soon. Glad we weren't subjected to that!

Veronica Graham-Brown (Howarth) Not much news this year, but it was so good to meet up with **Patricia Hedges** for lunch last summer. We hope to see each other again at the end of lockdown.

Patricia Hedges (Crowe) In spite of lockdown this has been an exciting year for me. My book about my mother's extraordinary life *The Raj, the Rolls and the Remorse* has received 5* reviews, and I am having an interview with Kate Delaney (of America Tonight Radio) this week. I have another book being published on March 31 - *Bark, Bark - this is my life - and it is yours too*. It is an uncomplicated philosophy book, written by a dog with a human voice. It's available through Amazon. More details from my website: *www.patriciahedges.com. (Patricia's website also gives her own life story, which is fascinating AP)*

Alison Maguire (Mason) Still alive and drowning in Scotland. Still unable to reach my flat in London. I am so pleased to hear about the Westonbirt garden renovations.

Section 24 (1954)

Section Representative:
Alison Robinson (De Courcy-Ireland)

I am, as always, very grateful to those of you who continue to keep in touch and respond to my pleas for news. I had feared that increasing age and infirmities, not to mention the difficulty of thinking of things to say in the midst of the monotony of lockdown, would mean fewer replies, so I am delighted that it didn't. Inevitably there has been sad news to report as well as a stoical acceptance of the limitations imposed on our lives during the past year.

Jenny Andrews (Clair) tragically lost her husband Barrie in January, after a long illness. Jenny was able to look after him at home and, with help from his daughters, kept him Covid-free. His funeral was held in the local church where their wedding had been blessed more than 25 years earlier, with his grandsons as bearers. Not surprisingly, Jenny is still feeling very tired as well as sad. *(I know I speak for all of us in sending you our love and sympathy, Jenny. You are much in our thoughts - AR).*

Elizabeth Bennett (Anning) says she is still here and grateful to be pretty *compos*, but has absolutely no news that will be different from anyone else suffering from lockdown lethargy. She says she has lost her zing but hopes to recover it in due course!

Elizabeth Ells (Rawlence) wrote that Covid and the lockdown have made surprisingly little difference to day to day life in their village at "the back of the north wind" in Ontario where there have been very few cases. However, as she speaks of "no travel at all, not even to see children and grandchildren within the province and absolutely no international travel", it sounds like the same sort of restrictions as in UK. Elizabeth sent an account by her sister **Mary Cave** about a time when the lake was frozen (see Section 34's news). She herself only remembers illicitly skating or sliding on a pond on the golf course and ending up soaked when the ice gave way!

Amelia Gardner (Langford) was saddened by the death of her younger sister **Elizabeth Abrahams** and not being able, because of lockdown regulations, to attend her funeral, or that of Elizabeth's husband shortly after. *(All of us who remember Lizzie share your sadness, Amelia - AR)* Amelia writes that living near the coast in Pembrokeshire has made lockdown easier and the rural setting suits their quiet lifestyle.

Caryll Green (Rees Reynolds) says she has no news worth sending in but is still alive and kicking!

Janet Knight (Sykes) also says she is still here. "It has been a strange year, not seeing or hearing from many friends, but I do hear from **Gillian Sandeman** and **Jennifer Smye (Nicholas)**, both friends from Sedgewick days!"

Sheena Mackenzie admired the photograph of the restored lake, commenting "I don't think I realised it had been created, just assumed it was always there, callow youth!" She says she has no news but is lucky to live in a condo building which most of the residents regard as their bubble, so spend time with each other, which decreases the loneliness. She misses the stimulation of playing bridge up to four times a week but was hoping her bridge club would be allowed to reopen sometime soon.

Sue Mitchell (Munro-Faure) agrees that not much has happened over the past year but feels she is lucky to live on the edge of a village and be able to go for walks with friends. Last summer was packed with visitors, during the relaxation in the lockdown, and the traffic was a nightmare, but they went out early and avoided the crowded places. Sue still hears from **Sylvia Lawrer (Farrer)** in New Zealand.

Val Moorby (Holmes-Johnson) wrote that she supposed "in true Westonbirt fashion we have all kept going and made the best of things" and was grateful that she, her family, and all but a couple of friends had avoided catching Covid.

Val herself has certainly managed to pack an amazing amount in to the year – mostly virtually! She has discovered the joys of Zoom, Facetime, WhatsApp etc (aided by family and advice from Mary Rusinow) and has been able to keep up not only with family and friends but with church services, talks, concerts, and her Italian group.

She misses going out for social events although during the summer respite she was able see some of her family and friends and enjoyed a few days in the Lakes with her brother. Her biggest disappointments have been the cancellation of her son's wedding in France (now planned for 2022) and not being able to see more of her two new great-grandchildren, although their parents keep her up to date with their progress. Val loved the Christmas Doors video sent out by the school and had also enjoyed a long phone chat with **Janet Knight.**

Heather Owen (Grange) had had her first vaccine jab when she wrote and was hopeful that the virus was receding after a grim year. She feels she is lucky to live in a cosy Cornish cottage, with a lovely garden, two daughters also in Cornwall, and with wonderful neighbours and a friendly village shop which stocks "everything and anything".

Heather thinks you can get used to anything: lockdowns, wearing masks, isolation etc and, like most of us, is grateful for emails and the telephone for keeping us in touch with family and friends – even those not heard from in a long time. She was sad to hear of **Lizzie Langford**'s death – "a sterling person" whom she met up with each year at the Association Meeting and was sorry that was cancelled this year. She does, however, keeps in touch with several WBs – **Bridget Frost**, **Alison Reed**, **Anna Grange**, **Ann Lewis**, and **Gill Hartigan** (plus her Section Representative!)

Alison Robinson (de Courcy-Ireland) has also been spending much time on Zoom and social media trying to keep in touch with family and friends. "Last year, we felt we were spending an increasing amount of time visiting friends in care homes or going to funerals. This year part of the sadness has been not being able to attend funerals or visit care homes.

"On a more cheerful note, in October we were able to spend a lovely few days in a rented cottage in the Wye Valley, together with the one daughter who lives in this country, before it was back to Zoom again. As a Samaritan, I count as an emergency worker, so have been able to continue doing my weekly shift. Understandably, the need is greater than ever – many of the calls being from the housebound or prisoners locked up for all but half an hour a day and, if on remand, waiting for 18 months or more for a trial date. And as well as putting one's own problems into perspective, it is good to get a change of scene and meet your fellow volunteer."

Mary Rusinow (Worthington)'s year began with Christmas and New Year in South Africa. She writes "My son-in-law had been UNICEF representative in Pretoria but was hauled back to headquarters in January. Accordingly, at least some of his siblings came for their last chance at a safari and we had four very good days in Pilanesberg and managed to see the Big Five.

I got back to Florida and the inevitable self-quarantine. The South African party eventually got out on an evacuation flight and joined Tamara's sister in The Hague where she is now working for her Dutch NGO. Her husband was finally able to join her but is not at all well and is on the list for a lung transplant. Not fun.

Dougal the dog and I did get to Italy for three months - there was no Covid in the village then - and got back to Florida in time to vote! Christmas in New York - Tamara was fifty, four days afterwards, very ageing! We are now back to self-quarantining, although I have had my first jab and hope to have the other next week."

The picture of the lake reminded Mary of sending for ice skates at least once during her time at school. "The ones I used dated from 1922 and belonged to my great-aunt. It was colder in those days - remember ice in the dormitory jugs?"

Gillian Sandeman (Wright) *(in Canada)* was feeling envious that her daughter in England (in her fifties) had had her first vaccine jab while Gillian and Sandy in their 80s will be lucky to get theirs by early April.

In an email at Christmas, Gillian had been hoping that their stay-at-home rule would end in February, but in March they were still more or less locked down even though Canadian infection rates and deaths were minor compared to UK. They are allowed to go out for walks and to the grocery store and are very grateful that the library has a kerb-side pick-up for books that have been ordered, so despite feeling quite isolated, they are both well and comfortable.

Their usual globe-trotting having been drastically constrained by the pandemic, they are hoping to get to Scotland and England in the autumn and are busy planning trips to the Orkneys (with Gillian's sister **Jennifer Pellow**), a few days in the Basque country followed by a wine cruise in the Bordeaux area, a wildlife viewing week in Hungary and Slovenia and a week-long cruise on the Caledonian Canal! Given how many trips got cancelled last year, Gillian says they will not be surprised if none of it happens! Meanwhile, when she wrote in early March, the morning temperature was -17°C and spring had definitely not arrived!

Section 23 (1953)

Section Representative:
Jean Stone (Borritt)

Jenny Botsford (Reynolds) I got lost off the system so have not contributed news for several years, so this is a bit of a catch up.

Downsizing from my house to a lovely garden flat two streets away, four years ago, was quite an upheaval, but it was so good that I moved then. About two years ago I was diagnosed with very aggressive Stage IV melanoma metastasised. However, with my brilliant consultant and new immunotherapy at the Royal Marsden Hospital my cancer is now "controlled", and I am able to live normally, albeit rather in the slow lane. A lot of the year I have been shielding and it is with great excitement when shielding stops, to go into a supermarket and actually choose one's own veg! I am on the board of directors of the limited company owning the 1935 Art Deco block which has nearly 200 flats. It has just had a £1.2 million internal refurbishment and I have been very involved with furnishing the foyer in 1935 style. I am also on the ward Conservatives committee and involved with local affairs. I see a lot of my family. Eldest son, Charles, who lives in Somerset, is frequently working in London. Younger son, Chris and wife Callie have a flat in Knightsbridge, and although they live in Hong Kong, were in Europe for a lot of the summer. Four of my grandchildren now live in London and others have made great efforts to see me, so I am very fortunate.

Several old girls are in close touch, my cousins **Diana Ford (Paxman)** and **Carol Lindsay Smith (Paxman), Penny Mann (Spurrell)** and **Laura Marks (Lister)**. Diana has recently moved to Wadhurst, very close to her daughter and family and Carol lives just off Columbia Road in London. We used to meet up a lot but Covid has prevented that.

Alas Penny is now very ill with cancer and is being looked after by her daughter, Frances (who was also at Westonbirt, as **Frances Mann**) and her husband in Cornwall. Penny's husband, Keith has their Kew house on the market and is going back and forth and will move to Cornwall. Despite the cancer, Penny is remarkably upbeat on our telephone calls. Laura unfortunately had a stroke several years ago, when she was so active in Warren, New South Wales, having been patron of the local hospital. She is quite disabled, but her brain and speech are fine.

My family's main excitement this year has been eldest granddaughter, Emily's wedding to James Davies. Although they had planned a big wedding in November with honeymoon hiking in Patagonia, that was clearly not to be. As her parents were in Europe, and feared if they went back to Hong Kong, they might not be able to get back, even for a small ceremony in November, it was decided to bring the wedding forward. We were so lucky. September 19th was the most brilliant, sunny day and thirty were allowed to attend. A flower bedecked St Paul's, Knightsbridge, was the setting where Em and James had got to know the delightful vicar quite well. We all sat in the chancel for a short but poignant service. Then walked out into the sun where the bride and groom were chauffeur driven round the block in a vintage Bentley as we walked to the Mandarin Oriental. All the young men looked so handsome in morning suits and the girls dressed in Ascot best with smart hats. It was such a brilliant change from the gloom of lockdown. Champagne on the terrace overlooking Hyde Park with a couple of excellent speeches was followed by a delicious sit-down lunch, with rather a lot of splendid wine and a funny speech from the best man.

Because the young had nowhere to go afterwards, a cocktail bar appeared in the corner after lunch, which proved extremely popular. My son told me I had to try the coffee martini, which I did, and it was delicious. Then he gave me a sip of his lychee martini and that was splendid too, so I had to have one of those. By the time grandson Max poured me into a taxi, I was extremely happy. Apparently one hundred martinis were drunk during the late afternoon!

Anne Greenstreet (Selby) Thanks so much for doing this for us! I was so sorry to see that **Elizabeth (Bubbles) Bale** had died. I am in touch with **Jenny Ewing (Wallace)** who lives in Wimbledon with her daughter and family. We have had rather a dull year, though the lovely summer weather meant we could see our family in the garden. My distanced birthday party had several separate groups!

Five grandchildren are homeschooling and two are at university, taught online so not quite dreaming spires! Preferable, however, to spending months in their bedrooms, and they both have a good group of flatmates. Eldest granddaughter works mainly from home, she lives in a shared house, but only a short distance from the family. Her sister has returned after being stuck in France for some months and is busy with A Level Physics as she hopes to go to university at last.

Anthony is nearly 93 and has a problem walking much, just potters about the house and garden. We have a splendid cleaner, gardener and food delivery so manage fine, with good neighbours. I have been joining some U3A and Arts Society meetings as well as church and a monthly meeting of a group of friends. We have had our first vaccination so hope to emerge soon if Boris allows.

Gillian Henson (Groome) also wrote saying, "At 85, I am grateful to have been able to actively join the family on a summer holiday to Falmouth, walking part of the south-west coastal path. Autumn found us back for a visit to Westonbirt Arboretum, far more stunning than the many times visited during school days. Even with tiers in place, we were able to all meet up for Christmas, a memorable time. Since then, nothing noteworthy."

Gillian is bubbled with a nearby daughter and her family and is still able to enjoy a game of mahjong with them, while waiting for better times. She is delighted that the Westonbirt lake has finally been restored after being such a depressing sight for so long and is grateful for the generosity of the OG *(old girl)* who enabled the work to take place.

Section 21 & 22 (1951 & 1952)

Section Representative:
Margot Gill (Wilcox)

Margot Gill (Wilcox) Thank you to those who have written in, it is much appreciated. All our lives have been changed because of Covid. I am in a bubble of one. The vicar has been great at having services on Facebook and emailing us to cheer us up. He also arranged people to ring those of us on our own, very thoughtful.

One piece of bad news for me is that my Peke, Mandy, died on her twelfth birthday. Have managed to rehome an ex-breeding bitch and she is a joy.

Glayne Greenaway (Rocyn-Jones) wrote to say that it has been a difficult year but that she has many local friends who help her, and her family in Paris and New Zealand are so good at keeping in touch. She says it was sad to hear of the death of **Liz Noyce, (Bubbles Clark)**, as they always met up on Reunion days and anniversaries. Recently she managed to speak to **Rosemary Mulholland (Hawkins,** known as **Hawkie**).

Susan Kavanagh (Harris) says that she has been confined to the UK because of the Covid restrictions and is with her daughter in Portsmouth. Her two granddaughters have returned to university to have room to study! Once restrictions are lifted, she will go back to California as she feels it is time to go before she is too old!

Ann Sadler (Millard) writes that lockdown has stopped just about everything that she usually does. She is still reasonably active, a bit arthritic and with a mild heart failure. Fortunately, her daughter lives five doors down the road and they are a bubble together, along with her next-door-neighbour who is a feisty 92! Three merry widows together.

Jane Sutton is well and active. In the break between the first and second lockdowns she managed to do a great deal of travelling in the UK, taking advantage of the coaches.

Jenifer Springett very kindly sent her form back to let us know that she is still with us.

Shirley Worlidge (Pryor) says they are both well and active and her husband is about to be 90, she is 87 with four children, seven grandchildren and a great-grandchild on the way.

Sections 19 and 20 (1949-50)

Section Representative:
Serena Jones

Sarah Abel (Poynor) My news of the lockdown year is limited. I broke my hip and have recovered well enough to live alone again, which I like, because I do not feel lonely and can keep myself motivated most of the time. My far-flung family keep an eye on me from a distance.

Susan Gardiner-Hill (Strachan) The situation is a bit lonely, but it's the same for all of us. Our news this year was the arrival of two great-granddaughters, both born last April. We had visits last summer and enjoyed them very much. Otherwise, the news is just ageing!

So glad to hear the lake has been mended - Westonbirt was such a happy and helpful experience for me.

Meriel Pickett (Sharpe) I have really enjoyed lockdown, because it has given me the opportunity to do all sorts of neglected jobs - finishing needlework, repairing china etc and, most fulfilling, getting the quite large garden into shape. I have 17 pots of iris reticulata and muscari coming into bloom now the snow has gone.

Jo, our youngest son, who runs the farm, comes in several times a week, and second son Hugh, who moved with his family to Woodchurch a year ago, comes when working in his kitchen (a catering business which he's setting up in an old farm building) just across the field.

I remember the Italian Gardens and the Camellia House and a magnolia stellata by the lake - so many wonderful trees. One year we had a foot of snow, and borrowed tin trays from the kitchen to go sledging down to the lake. With hindsight I wish we had seen more of the Arboretum - happy days.

Beryl Thorp (Holm) Like everyone, this last year has been very different to all the others. I was ill before Christmas 2019, so booked a cruise to the Canaries where I looked forward to some sunshine and having a rest. The first day out I fell and broke my hip so was airlifted to Spain and, after surgery, came back to hospital in England followed by a stay in a nursing home. I eventually got home just before the first lockdown.

Since then, I have been shielded so have not been in a shop for a year. However, I have some helpful friends and neighbours and have learnt how to do click and deliver as well as Zoom for a variety of talks, meetings etc. I am sure that this is no different to many others, but I think we oldies have managed well! I am now looking forward to my ninetieth birthday in a few days' time and plan a party in the summer - hopefully. I am about to have a my second Covid jab and optimistically have booked a hair appointment.

I was very interested to read about the wonderful work done on the lake. It looks lovely. It was always one of my favourite areas in the gardens. I recall the very cold snowy winter of 1946/7, when the lake froze over, and we were allowed to go skating on it - great fun!

Elisabeth Wells (Burt) Like many of us, I am locked in and thankful for a garden to get out into. I get so much pleasure from the garden birds. I am in touch with **Joy Willey**, who phones, and we look forward to meeting up. Full marks to Serena who works so hard to keep us all going. *(Thank you! SJ)*

Elizabeth Wicks (Butcher) What a strange year and a ghastly one for some. I am so lucky that all is well with my family. Daughters, Lalu and Joanna, have been to see me, one from Taunton and one from London, whenever allowed. It was a real highlight seeing them in their homes for four nights in each. Both came for my birthday and we were able to go out to a good pub for lunch - such a joy and no lockdown.

"Our Place Wye" is a great organisation which supplies help, if needed, including shopping. Thank heaven I have mostly been able to do my own. It's been fun having friends in for tea or coffee.

I was able, in the summer, to have a session of Pilates in the garden with a superb teacher, and hope classes can start again soon. Wye is a gorgeous place for walking sometimes with friends. We've been so lucky with the weather.

Facetime with my delightful granddaughter has been fun. She can work from home in Sadler's Wells. Being no technologist, I am so grateful for my telephone but do realise that email etc, if I'd been a typist instead of a nurse, would have helped me a lot!

I think that some of the aspects of this last year have definitely brought me back to 1939 and the Second World War. My home was in the Yorkshire Dales, not far from Skipton. We lived a mile and a half from a bus stop. Petrol was highly rationed so bikes, or a horse and trap, were very much in demand! I bussed and walked to school. Instead of face masks we had a gas mask always with us. We slept with them near our beds. Food was rationed and in short supply. Sugar, eggs, butter, meat, sweets, oranges, lemons, bananas - if lucky one a month. We had hens - wonderful! No deep freezes but eggs, if too many, were kept in "water glass" and taken out when needed in the hope they weren't bad! Clothes were rationed and we had coupons which were shared between the family - boys apparently grew quicker than girls.

There was much sadness and fear since the war office would send word, ie "missing, believed killed". A wonderful girl I knew lost two brothers in three weeks. Those living in towns and cities did have, I think, a more fearful time because of air raids etc. Walking, biking, horse and trap, and haymaking in the nearby farm kept us fit. There were new ways of living after the war and people helped one another, so like it is now.

Keep well everyone and smile if you can. Westonbirt is flourishing and I loved it. Here's to 2022 and the hope we can meet with a few friends remaining in Sections 18,19, 20 and more.

Joy Willey (Crowe) I can't say I have suffered too much by being locked down as, like all old people living alone one, is accustomed to making one's own amusements. I do miss visits from the family and especially the granddaughters staying on their exeats etc.

Being near my daughter I can be in a bubble with her family, although we have been very careful as her boy sees his friends. Fortunately, I can do a lot of Zoom and have heard many interesting lectures I wouldn't otherwise have, so much easier than going out on a cold night.

As a result of my entry last year, I have been in touch with **Pat Crowe**, not my contemporary but someone who has led such an interesting and productive life.

At Christmas I spoke to **Elisabeth Wells (Burt)** and also speak every now and then to **Sylvia McDougald (Field)**. Sadly no one else is still around.

I am hoping there will be a Speech Day this year as my last granddaughter at the school is leaving and there won't be the same contact there has been with Westonbirt. Being Games Captain, this should have been the culmination of her school career, but so much of it has been spent at home! Even when at school, no matches. She was offered captaincy of the Scottish Under-19 lacrosse team but there have been no matches or training there either! The school have been marvellous though, keeping up the online teaching, not easy for the staff, I am sure.

Sadly, no travels to report but better luck next year I hope.

Sections 17 and 18 (1947-48)

Section Representative:
Pauline Jackson (Garrett)

Jennifer Barton enjoyed her ninetieth birthday last year when her cousins brought everything for a celebratory lunch in her garden in Selsey. This is where she spent the first lockdown – the local support was magnificent, and she was able to spend time outdoors trying to control the flourishing weeds! Jennifer returned to London just before Christmas where she has caught up with delayed appointments and had a chance to clear out family papers etc.

She cooks using minimal effort and has been trying unexpectedly tasty air-packed dishes! She also relies on deliveries of fruit and veg – not the ideal alternative to shopping, but legs not allowing her to walk very far. Jennifer enjoys watching Freeview television, especially BBC4, although generally falls asleep during the evening.

She feels fortunate in being retired and able to carry on tolerably normally. She says that she would have given up golf long ago anyway. Jennifer is hoping for everyone and the economy's sake that things pick up soon.

Josephine Daszkiewicz (Woodward) is settled and happy living in Yorkshire. She is always interested in reading the mailings sent out by the school.

Jean Edwards (Wates) lives at home with the help of a carer. Three of her nine grandchildren are now married, and she has one great-grandchild on the way. Two more weddings are planned for this year. Only one grandchild, a chef, is furloughed. The others are working from home, except a doctor who has been working on the Oxford vaccine. Home, in two cases, is New York – so weekly zoom sessions!

Rosemary Francis (Walton) I spoke to Rosemary's carer, who tells me that Rosemary is well and living in her beautiful home in Herefordshire. She has a wonderful family which includes great-grandchildren.

Gylla Godwin (Latham) is happily living in London. She has a home with a small back garden that fronts the Thames. When she moved there some years ago, she had a weeping willow planted and every year in the spring she gets much pleasure in looking out in her garden as the foliage starts to appear. She also watches the activity on the river. Gylla still has a lot of interest in the Garden History Society, now part of the Gardens Trust. She has happy memories of her time living in North Devon.

Primrose Minney appreciates receiving the Westonbirt Association News each year. She was interested to read about the restoration of the lake at Westonbirt, and that the school has now become co-educational. At what she classes as her advanced age (92), she is the same age as the school! Primrose lives quietly, with her tortoiseshell rescue cat Pebbles, and enjoys gardening when the weather is right. Unfortunately, Primrose's relatives do not live nearby.

Anne Moutrie (Venn) lives at home but is now confined to her bed. She still enjoys receiving the Westonbirt Association News.

Section 16 (1946)

Section Representative:
Jane Reid

Acknowledgement of the 2021 January Newsletter was received from **Patricia Krichauff (Faulkner).**

Elizabeth Watson (Allen) What a year! I came back from Portugal mid-March 2020. Exactly one week later I went down with Covid, fortunately very mildly and with no after-effects. So now have been in lockdown for a year. Plenty to do in the house, half-finished tapestry, an impossible jigsaw, cooking, and painting towards an exhibition in October, which sadly will be the last I do.

No plans for any holidays. I haven't seen any of my family for over a year so will be doing the rounds. I hope that everyone in our section has kept well and found plenty to do and had enough Zooms!

Newsletters were sent by post to the other six active members of Section 16; none were returned as undeliverable.

Sections 13, 14 and 15 (1943-45)

Section Representative:
Serena Jones

Gillian Blum (Gregory) Not a lot of news due to the lockdown, but I try to keep busy and have done two large jigsaws with another one on the go. I read and do crosswords. Recently I celebrated my 95th birthday which, in spite of everything, was very enjoyable.

Rosemary Campbell (Fraser) The greatest highlight of this past year was a four day visit to the Nare Hotel, near St Mawes in Cornwall, for my 94th birthday. A long drive down, but it is a really wonderful place to stay. I was with my daughter, Catherine, who was marvellous looking after me. I had my own bedroom and bathroom across the landing from Catherine, so she was able to pop across and help me dress etc. The night of my birthday, at supper, the staff sang "Happy Birthday" - such a treat, and the other guests joined in - so kind.

I can walk with a frame, or I get pushed in a wheelchair. Everyone there was so kind and helpful. The hotel looks straight out onto the sea, with a garden outside full of flowers, and a comfortable sitting room.

Mercia MacDermott (Adshead) The past year has been a strange and difficult time for all of us, but I feel that my problems and deprivations have been immeasurably less severe than those of younger age groups, whose education, careers, incomes and normal activities have been so cruelly blighted.

2020 was my 94th year, so staying at home was not such a burden. I have plenty of books and am able to indulge in my retirement interests, which include geology and archaeology. A wonderful neighbour does my weekly shopping for me and I am sufficiently mobile to be able to go out alone for walks. My home is not far from the sea, so I can walk on the prom and the beach, or go to the local Marine Gardens. I live on the eighth floor of a tower block and, on a clear day, I can see the Isle of Wight to the west and Beachy Head to the east, as well as the turbines of the wind farm in the channel some eight miles out to sea.

Having seen much of the world (with high spots that include Venice, Mount Fuji, the Kremlin, Lake Baikal, the Taj Mahal, the Grand Canyon, the Pyramids and Uluru), I had already decided to confine my travelling to coach trips in Britain, so I am so much luckier than younger people longing to travel abroad. I do miss having coffee and tea with friends, although we keep in touch by phone, and I miss the activities of our local National Trust Association and the Friends of Worthing Museum. My greatest hardship is having to do without my cleaning lady!

It is not often that one feels glad that one is old, rather than young but, as I said, we live in strange times!

Sections 1-12 (1931-42)

Serena Jones (Sections 1-8), Pauline Jackson (Section 9), Rebecca Willows (Sections 10-12)

There are no active members in Sections 1–8, and no news from Sections 9 and 12). There is the following news from Section 11).

Ann Durrant (Griffiths) wrote that hearing about the lake reminded her of the time her friend, **Jenny Bishop,** and she boated out on a lilo. They were having such fun, they completely forgot about roll-call! She continues that she escaped the sixth form, saying she had to do war work. She worked at the Army Remount Department in Melton Mowbray looking after the horses of the Household Cavalry and the Blues and Royals.

Since then she married, had four children, and was a magistrate for 30 years. She wrote "Now aged 96, I am wobbling on. My sister, **Madge**, now living in Australia, is 98 and still going!"

And finally... are you decluttering?

To those of you who have made it to this page, and who may be having a clear-out due to downsizing or moving house, or who have spent part of the Covid lockdowns decluttering, here is a plea for you to donate any unwanted old copies of the News, or any school memorabilia, for the archives.

Please send any donations to Mrs Rhiannon Roche, Head of Public Relations and Events, at the School. If in doubt, please phone her first on 01666 880333, to check that what you are offering would be welcomed.

Invitation to Westonbirt Association Members

Westonbirt School always welcomes alumnae, whether on formal occasions such as Association Days, or for informal visits to reminisce about your school days. We would ask, in the interests of security, and to make sure we are able to welcome you on your preferred date, that you contact **Mrs Rhiannon Roche**, via her school email address, *rhiannon.roche@westonbirtschool.uk* or by telephoning her on 01666 880333. This is especially important under the current Covid restrictions.

There's always something new to see, in terms of academic and extra-curricular activities, new buildings and projects to restore the old, and current pupils are always fascinated to meet their predecessors. You are also very welcome to bring your family, even if you have no daughters or granddaughters to follow in your academic footsteps!

Whether or not you plan to visit the school in person, you may also like to visit our website, *www.westonbirt.org,* which is constantly being updated with school news and photos, and has a picture gallery from the archives.

How to Contact the Westonbirt Association

The Westonbirt Association database is kindly managed by the School, and so the School is now your first point of contact for any enquiries regarding the Association. **Mrs Rhiannon Roche,** will be able to direct you to the most appropriate person, according to the nature of your query. She will also be able to provide contact details for your Section Representative, whose personal information is no longer included in the News Magazine for the sake of their privacy.

Incidentally, please don't forget to let **Rhiannon** know if your own contact details change, so that we can keep you informed of Association matters and can find you if any of your former classmates are looking for you. If you're a fan of social media, you may also enjoy networking via on the alumni Facebook page: *www.facebook.com/groups/108986984329/*

Rhiannon works at the school full time, year-round, so is generally available during office hours. You may reach her via the main school telephone number, 01666 880333, or by emailing her at *rhiannon.roche@westonbirtschool.uk* She is always glad to hear from past pupils.

How to Order Copies of the Westonbirt Association News

Since 2015, to gain efficiencies, save costs, and to take advantage of advances in modern technology, we have changed the way we produce and distribute the Westonbirt Association News.

If you are a regular subscriber, you are welcome to go on receiving your copy as before, despatched by the News Finances and Distribution Officer, Jenny Webb, for as long as your account with her is in sufficient credit.

However, you will also now be able to order the latest edition, and all future editions, online, wherever you live in the world. Your copy will be printed in your local territory and sent at local postage rate. If you do this while your account with Jenny is still in credit, she will refund the balance on request - or if you prefer, you may simply donate the balance to the Westonbirt Association Memorial Bursary Fund.

If you prefer not to order online, you may also be able to order a print copy from your local high street bookshop by providing them with the ISBN number of the latest edition.

If, on the other hand, you are one of the many people who prefer these days to read ebooks, you may prefer to order an ebook version, which will be made available via all the mainstream ebook platforms, including Kindle, Kobo and iBooks.

We are confident that this is the best way forward for the long-term interests of the Association, and we hope it will also appeal to the younger generation (and many of the older ones!) who enjoy using digital technology. Please be assured, however, that we will always produce print copies for those who prefer them, and also for our substantial Association News archive.

Westonbirt Association Memorial Bursary Fund

The Westonbirt Association Memorial Bursary was set up in the late 1940s in memory of the five former Westonbirt pupils who lost their lives during the Second World War while they were members of the Forces, Civil Defence or the Nursing Services.

The aim of the fund is to give a bursary each year to help fund the school fees of girls at the school. The Memorial Bursary is still running today, and each year the Association makes an award from this fund to help towards the sixth form fees of one or more pupils.

To be considered for the Memorial Bursary, girls must be nominated by the school in the spring of their Year 11. Candidates complete an application form and are interviewed by a panel from the Westonbirt Association Committee. The process provides good experience for later job and university applications, and, for the successful candidate, receipt of the award enhances their CV as well as providing welcome financial help. Once awarded, payment is made for both years of the recipient's sixth form.

Over the years, we have helped more than eighty pupils in this way. With income levels from investments so low at present, and school fees rising, new donations are always welcome to increase the value of the award.

How to Donate to the Memorial Bursary Fund

Cash donations

Payments may be made by cheque payable to "Westonbirt School" and should be clearly marked for the Westonbirt Association Memorial Bursary Fund.

Online by standing order

Please reference payment in the following format:

Account name: Westonbirt School
Sort code: 200384
Account number: 30951927
Bank: Barclays

Bequests

As the school is a charity, bequests are free from liability to inheritance tax. The following are suitable words to send to your solicitor with a request that the Westonbirt Association Memorial Bursary be included in your will:

"I bequeath to Westonbirt School in the county of Gloucestershire the sum of £x, free of duty, to be used for the purposes of the Westonbirt Association Memorial Bursary."

You might also wish to inform the school as follows:

"I intend to make a bequest to the school for the purposes of the Westonbirt Association Memorial Bursary."

GiftAid Declaration for the Westonbirt Association Memorial Bursary

If you are a UK taxpayer, the school can reclaim tax on any gifts you make, via the Gift Aid scheme, provided you fill in the declaration form below in full and return it with your first gift.

Please treat as Gift Aid donations all qualifying gifts of money made *(please circle as applicable)*: *today / in the past 4 years / in the future.*
I enclose a donation of £.......... as a contribution to the Westonbirt Association Memorial Bursary.

I confirm I have paid or will pay an amount of income tax or capital gains tax for each tax year (6 April to 5 April) that is at least equal to the amount of tax that Westonbirt School and all other charities that I donate to will reclaim on my gifts for that tax year. I understand that other taxes such as VAT and council tax do not qualify. I understand the charity will reclaim 25p on every £1 that I give on or after 6 April 2021

Title______________ Forename ____________________________________

Surname____

Address____

Postcode____

Signature____

Date____

Please notify Westonbirt School if you want to cancel this declaration OR change your name or home address OR no longer pay sufficient tax on your income and/or capital gains. If you pay income tax at the higher or additional tax rate and want to receive the additional tax relief due to you, you must include all your Gift Aid donations on your self-assessment tax return.

Please send donations and the completed form to:
The Finance Manager, The Bursary, Westonbirt School
Tetbury, Gloucestershire GL8 8QG
Registered Charity Number 311715

We would like to thank Alanbrookes Ltd
for kindly auditing the Association's accounts.

Lightning Source UK Ltd.
Milton Keynes UK
UKHW022107230721
387663UK00010B/484

9 781911 223771